AWAKENED BY

HEART-FIRE

Wildland Fire Stories

and the Secrets to the Universe

Thomas M. Wurm

This book is not intended as a substitute for the medical advice of physicians. The reader should regularly consult a physician in matters relating to his/her health, particularly with respect to any symptoms that may require diagnosis or medical attention.

Mountain Mind Tricks Publishing

ISBN-978-0-578-64825-5

Printed in the United States of America

I would like to dedicate this book to the the Infinity-Fire

ACKNOWLEDGMENTS

I am eternally grateful to my wife, Dorea, for always supporting me as I adventured to become a published author.

I will also never forget the time and patience that Brett Lewis—my acupuncturist, shaman, and mentor—gave me through the emotional rollercoasters that I found myself on as I wrote this book. Thank you for helping me see myself with clarity and for giving me the foundation to stand on as a coach and mentor for others.

MOUNTAIN MIND TRICKS

Powerful Coaching—to change the world one heart at a time

To thank you for buying my book,
I have included a FREE meditation accompaniment series!

Download it here:

http://bit.ly/Heart-Fire-Meditations-Folder

HELP ME HELP YOU!

Please Leave a
Book Review on Amazon!

If you bought this book, please support your independent author and leave an honest review on Amazon! Your reviews are invaluable to me as they help make my future books even better!

Thank you in advance,
Thomas M. Wurm

YOUR CALL-TO-ACTION

If you want to transform your life through soul consciousness, please contact me for more information!

Website: https://www.mountainmindtricks.com/
Email: Transformation_Specialist@MountainMindTricks.com

Only reach out if you are truly committed to enacting positive change in your life!

Many Blessings,
Thomas M. Wurm

Thomas M. Wurm

Thomas Wurm is a *wildland firefighter, author, coach, speaker, and business owner.* With danger waiting around every corner, his fire career guided him to see the true nature of life. Thomas used what he learned on the fireline and applied it to self-help and spiritualism with the powerful intention of helping others be *healthy, safe, and happy.*

Thomas uses co-active coaching methodology, hypnosis, NLP/MER (guided meditation), nutrition, and fitness as tools for success in his practice. Thomas is a Transformation Specialist and studied at the Awakened Academy, International NLP Center, International Sports Science Association, Self-Publish School, Empowerment Partnership, and on the fireline in the western United States.

Thomas lives with his wife and dogs in the rugged mountains of Montana's Bitterroot Valley. In his spare time, Thomas enjoys backpacking in the mountains, splitboarding in the winter, and fly fishing in the summer, all while finding inspiration in nature to practice photography or to ignite an idea for his next book. If

Thomas isn't in the backcountry, he is most likely on an adventure somewhere around the globe!

If you want to connect with Thomas M. Wurm (and stay informed on any upcoming publications), please visit: www.MountainMindTricks.com

CONTENTS

Glossary   3

Preface   5

Prologue: How a Wildland Firefighter Found the
Infinity-Fire   11

PART ONE: THE EAST—REMEMBER HEART-FIRE

1. Heart-Fire Basics   33

2. Wildland Firefighting with My Gut   45

3. Awakened by Heart-Fire   63

4. Fire Inside Me   69

5. Infinity-Fire Alliance   77

PART TWO: THE SOUTH—IGNITE HEART-FIRE

6. Heart-Fire Safety   87

7. Mind-Body-Spirit Purification   97

8. Detoxify Your Heart   107

9. Heart-Fire Guidance for Fear Versus Love   117

PART THREE: ACTIVATE HEART-FIRE

10. Infinity-Fire in Action   125

11. Heart-Fire Method   129

12. Journey to the West   157

Conclusion   161

Afterword   165

Endnotes   167

AWAKENED BY
HEART-FIRE

Wildland Fire Stories
and the Secrets to the Universe

GLOSSARY

Infinity-Fire	God
Heart Fire	Chinese medicine constitution
Heart-Fire	Soul
Heart-Fire Embrace	Owning that you are your highest-self, right now
Compassion	Kindness driven by love and understanding
Unconditional Love	Devotion to another's well-being no matter what they think, feel, do, or believe
Triangle of Self-Love	The foundation of all spiritual work, the triangle of self-love is supported by nourishment (breath, water, food, exercise, sleep), deep love (self-love, love for others and all beings), and accountability (staying on course with your action plan)
Triangle of Conviction	Confidence, clarity, and certainty
Triangle of Spiritual Power	Alignment of yourself, your highest-self, and the Infinity-Fire

Infinity-Fire Alliance — Alignment of the three triangles of self-love, conviction, and spiritual power

Flow — A state of awareness that arises when partaking in a task that is just challenging enough but can be carried out with ease. The body takes over all action, and time and thinking disappear.

Dharma — The state of following your soul's purpose to allow yourself to live a life of flow and ease free from chaos. You and the universe are aligned toward achieving a mission.

Kundalini Awakening — An ancient Indian term used in yoga to describe an electric energy moving from the base of the spine up to the head. This electric shock blows open the crown chakra creating a mystical experience or the sensation of being touched by God.

Fractal — A geometric pattern that repeats on all scales

Law of Attraction — Vibrations liking and finding similar vibrations

I came into this world with a curiosity that couldn't be quenched by anything earthly. I became a Chātra (which means "seeker" in Hindi) when I was born. I have always been connected to the spirit realm, but my connection seemed to wax and wane like the undulations of a wave. At the crest of the wave, my connection with spirit would be strong for years at a time. However, something would inevitably throw me off course for a while, my curiosity would diminish, and I would live in the trough of the wave at its lowest point.

With every wave and cycle of spiritual connection I grew closer to the divine only to be pulled away once again from my spiritual parent. During a high point in one of my spiritual cycles, I found the "four directions" teachings of Native Americans. The four directions explain cycles in terms of a wave pattern. Everything in the universe starts in the East and is in the direction of creation. Following creation is action, learning, and growth in the South. After a Chātra has learned enough to satisfy their heart and soul, they move into the West. The world of the West is a place where one can use personal experiences to teach others. After some time, a Chātra may move into the North where they become an elder and knowledge-keeper in the spiritual realm while developing deeper relationships with the physical and spiritual worlds. A healing crisis forced me to move from the East to the South and these are the teachings that brought me transformation on all levels.

In this book I use the term Infinity-Fire which to me means God, Universal Consciousness, Great Spirit, Spirit, Spiritual Sun, Higher Power, or Spiritual Parent. I utilize my own term as I am reluctant to use the word "God" because of the religious connotations and potential to incite divisiveness. In my view, all religions and all cultures are talking about the same Higher Power, just in their own cultural context. So, to stay away from confusion and religious connotations, I will use the term Infinity-Fire to encompass all cultures and religions because anyone and everyone should have comfortable access to this knowledge.

The Infinity-Fire is the place from which golden healing light originates and this is where I received all of the teachings in this book. The concepts in this book came to me during deep coaching sessions with my acupuncturist, during meditations, or as a sudden download in my dreams. I turned my heart space into a communication center with the Infinity-Fire through meditation, calming my mind enough to truly listen. Communication occurred when my heart was open enough to receive messages from the Infinity-fire.

Unconditional Love is such a common term, but ubiquity tends to promote the meaninglessness of familiarity. To be clear, my definition of Unconditional Love is: absolute devotion to someone regardless of what they think, feel, or believe. Compassion sits in the same bath water, as my definition is: the unwavering concern for others' suffering to the point that the concern becomes a driving force for action. In simpler terms compassion is love plus understanding. These feelings of unconditional love and compassion carry a frequency and vibration that are key to opening your heart space to the Infinity-Fire. (A vibration is a wave pattern in energy or an oscillation between highs and lows in a wave. The frequency is the rate of change between highs and lows.) You need both vibration and frequency to match the energy of the Infinity-Fire to facilitate a Heart-Fire communication. The simplest way to achieve this is through feeling whole body unconditional love and compassion.

Communication with the Infinity-Fire is possible because we all have a piece of it in our heart-space, also known as our soul. I use the term Heart-Fire to describe the concept of a soul and the way in which our soul has the ability to communicate with its higher Infinity-Fire. This fire in your heart differs from a fire you see on a physical landscape as it does not consume life, but rather, it supports it. Heart-Fire is life-giving and supports the expansion of unconditional love and compassion. It is the unique and divine spark that rests inside every single person's heart-space.

This book's *mission* is to systematically move you closer to unconditional love and compassion as this is the higher vibration that allows all lower forms of vibration to flow away. After experiencing this book, your end-state is to awaken to your true nature as a spiritual being that has, for a time, chosen an earthly body to learn lessons that cannot be learned in higher dimensions. The *task* in this book is to move you into a daily practice of using your Heart-Fire to communicate with the Infinity-Fire so you can carry out your original instruction. (I call this the Heart-Fire Method.) The *purpose* of finding and completing your original instruction is to help spread more unconditional love and compassion throughout humanity. (I call this the soul's purpose.) We all have a unique way of manifesting this purpose because we all have an individual piece of Heart-Fire with specific instructions.

Your soul's purpose is required learning that you need in order to advance your spirit into the next vibrational phase of existence. The law of attraction is best described as vibrations liking similar vibrations. If there are two tuning forks of similar vibrations on a table and you strike one of the tuning forks, the other one will start vibrating at the same frequency![1] This is the exact same idea as tuning your Heart-Fire into unconditional love and compassion. By carrying this vibration with you, you are spreading the vibration to others and changing the world around you. Your specific vibrational frequency also attracts the same vibrations, thus establishing the essence of the law of attraction. Positive emotions attract positive outcomes! In other words, carrying a higher vibration like unconditional love and compassion will, by universal law, help you manifest your true bliss, happiness, abundance, beauty, and love. Specifically, for some time my soul's purpose was to be a wildland firefighter. I needed to see fire in its rawest form in order to understand my spiritual journey. I am a student of fire and the Heart-Fire skills are my lessons. I will impart to you what I have learned from wildland firefighting spirituality.

What my wildland fire career has taught me more than anything is that there is nothing more important than love for self, love for others, and love for the planet. As a wildland firefighter I have spent the last thirteen years tending the forest floor with a chainsaw, cleaning out the dead, young, and sick trees to make way for more vibrant and genetically healthier trees. I helped make room for more elk and lynx, and even improved owl hunting conditions, while I yelled, "Face cut!" and felled trees day after day. (A face cut is a wedge-shaped cut in a tree in the direction you intend to fall it.) Every day spent in the woods picking off ticks, getting saw gas on my hands and on my lunch, dodging trees, and stacking sticks to burn later in the name of ecological management have been a source of strength for me. Through my journey, I have realized that this ecological pruning has a been a gigantic metaphor for ecology of the human experience. Ecology can be applied to the woods, but I applied it to myself as a wildland fire leader, a firefighter, and a Chātra. It is important to have good ecology because holistic health of an ecosystem is good for self, good for others, and good for the planet. In the end, you are an ecosystem and you are looking for better ecology, aren't you?

How a Wildland Firefighter
Found the Infinity-Fire

I have spent the last thirteen years fighting wildland fires from Alaska to Texas, across the coast ranges in California, and to the snowy Tetons. I have seen fire and what it can do to forcibly fabricate a blank canvas on the landscape or completely ruin lives. I have watched my margins for error shrink as I stared my own mortality in the face. I have watched billions of dollars in effort go down the drain while suppressing fires that didn't want to succumb to the demands of humans. Through my work, I have lit off thousands of acres to restore critical habitats and to restore fire's regenerative benefits to the ecosystem. I have witnessed fires grow from a single tree to thousands of acres in hours.

When my margin for error was the smallest it's ever been, I experienced a close call during a dry August day in Southeast Idaho. I was staffing a type six engine (a firetruck with three firefighters and six hundred gallons of water in addition to everything needed to survive for two weeks) and there was a lightning storm that rolled through the Idaho Falls desert. The

11

crackling bolts ignited upwards of fifteen fires in the same area. We were immediately dispatched due to the high fire danger, and the smokejumpers (firefighters that jump from planes) were the first emergency personnel to be launched. As we drove out of Idaho Falls, we rounded the corner on the outskirts of town and the highway opened up to lava rock and rolling sage. (Lava rock is a firetruck tire's worst nightmare and the landscape of this area was teeming with it.) Through the windshield I noticed a column of black smoke in the distance which was a clear indicator that we wouldn't be returning home that night. Realizing my evening plans would have to wait, I enjoyed the surging feeling of comradery triggered by the smell of the smoke that only fire brothers and sisters know.

As we got closer to the fire, we watched the lawn darts (a slang term for smokejumpers) circle the smoke in their plane and drop ribbons to test the air currents before they kicked out the rookie firefighters. We drove another thirty minutes toward the smoke, loudly blaring music to mask the nerves we knew we all felt, before we arrived at the staging area (the initial location to safely receive our briefings and game plan).

When we arrived at the fire, bulldozers were working a flank with the smokejumpers lighting fire behind the bulldozers in an effort to box in and contain the blaze. The other flank was being worked by air attack (the person in charge of the air resources circling in a plane high in the sky) with the help of six small engine retardant planes. (Picture something akin to crop dusters with the craziest pilots ever and then add in the unpredictability of fire and you'll get the picture!) Our unit was synced with the smokejumpers near the head of the fire. Their operational plan was standard, and everything seemed to be going perfectly. We were getting close to hooking around the head of the fire and achieving full containment. There was one remaining ninety-degree corner left to make with the firing operation (strategically lighting fire to burn the landscape's fuel on our own terms before the wildfire came). But, as any good firefighter knows, ninety-degree corners have to be taken very seriously because fire will exploit a corner at all costs.

Our engine and another engine started to burn off the last corner, working in opposite directions in order to catch the head of the fire. We could see the main fire-front moving in our direction at a good clip, with forty-foot flame lengths ripping off sagebrush along the way. This was one of those times that there was no question that it was time for us to burn—it was going to be a relatively short distance of fire for us to put down, maybe a quarter mile at most. As wildfire operations go, it should have been a simple and straightforward task; something we'd all done a million times. The second our truck began the firing operation, a dust devil arose and blasted our test fire. In a split second, our ten-by-ten test fire surged into forty-foot flame lengths all around us. It didn't take long to realize we were in critical danger! We screamed and yelled, "Get in the truck; let's go, let's go!" I will never forget the moment that I looked at the Engine Boss and asked, "Knock down hose?" (A knock down hose is the last defense hose for truck protection. If it's under consideration, it's like asking, "We're dead, right?") We jumped into the engine with our fire packs, tools, and drip torches (spouted canteens specifically designed to safely carry fire), and the Engine Boss put the pedal to the floor. We traveled on a dozer line, only able to drive five miles an hour, and all of our heads bounced off the roof as we rushed over the rough terrain. The fire moved around fifteen miles an hour on both sides of us, and we had no other choice but to outrun it. I remember the heat blasting through the windows and burning my ears, and I used my glove to block the heat from my face. I recall praying and asking for help as I was faced with my mortality in a real way for the first time. With some luck, we eventually outran the fire, but our firing operation ballooned from a ten-by-ten test fire to ten thousand acres in just a few hours. As we defeatedly ate our lunch that afternoon, we sang "Another One Bites the Dust" and watched the fire from afar. It was in that moment that I saw the deeper meaning of fire and realized that fire is not inanimate—it has a spirit. I came close enough to the raw power of fire that day to feel it. (As I write this, I can feel the searing heat on my ears all over again, and my gut churns with uncertainty.) It's a reminder every day that life is short, and we have to be grateful for every moment we have.

I continued to carry this new knowledge about fire with me throughout my wildland firefighting career. Fire indeed has a spirit—it's alive and can choose what it wants to do. Fire will burn wherever the fuel continuity allows; it flows like water in a brisk wind and it climbs mountains with ease. Fire will find drainage locations and run with them with shocking speed. It can climb a ridge to catch the helpful tendrils of the wind and it can throw scouting embers to assess nearby conditions to ignite new spots. In essence, fire will grow multiple heads to more easily find and devour its next meal. A fire with enough momentum can and will create its own weather.

Fire is the manifestation of the great recycler and destroyer, and I feel blessed to have witnessed the Hand of God in the wilderness changing the landscape and wiping the slate clean. There is nothing like hearing a flame-front coming like a freight train through the forest; the sound of crashing trees and roaring combustion makes your heart race with primal fear and awe.

When I watched fires work their way through lush forests or scream across grasslands, I observed its behavior; I studied it. I am a student of fire not just as a fireman, but also as a spiritual being. Fire is my element; it is my ally. Fire has taught me that everything has consciousness, and this is how Native Americans see the world. Every animal, every rock, every blade of grass has consciousness. The most beautiful thing I have ever seen in life is a grass fire at night moving up a drainage and rolling in perfect lines over ridges. At night, fire is bewildering, mesmerizing, and you can't comprehend how absolutely beautiful it is without seeing it for yourself. Our modern world carries the stigma that all fire is bad, and this is completely wrong. *Fire is the spirit of renewal, destruction, and rebirth.* Fire is the provider for the landscape; it recycles the old while creating a path for new life in a natural ecosystem. Humans have personally felt this terror in man-made ecosystems as recent mega fires have ravaged neighborhoods and destroyed homes, and my heart truly goes out to them.

I have seen fire burn out tree roots as it looks for the deepest possible solution to its hungry search for fuel. I have seen fires burn around wet drainages, later hooking to go where it wants in a breathtaking exhibition of perseverance. Fire has patience and, given time, fire will always go where it wants. Even when it seems as if victory is in the hands of the firefighter, fire can and will be back on its own terms—it will return with a vengeance to get what it wants.

In the ecosystems of planet Earth, the elements of fire, water, earth, and air are the only constants. It doesn't matter the interval of elapsed time between a wildland fire; the landscape will see fire. Every ecosystem has a fire regimen—the pattern, frequency, and intensity of wildfires that prevail in an area over long periods of time. Fire is part of the natural processes, just as water is known to erode earth. All landscapes yearn for fire just as your heart yearns for the flameless fire. The Heart-Fire I refer to in this book is flameless and doesn't consume in the same way as real fire—it supports life, unconditional love, and compassion; it is divine in nature. Your Heart-Fire is what will bring you unconditional love, compassion, and fulfilled dreams. Heart-Fire skills differ from those found in any book, online course, or from any guru, and no technique will guide you like the Heart-Fire Method because your Heart-Fire is yours alone and only your Heart-Fire knows where it wants to burn. Only your spirit can see the continuity of possibilities and burn past any obstacle or challenge.

I used my Heart-Fire skills on wildland fire assignments to sense danger, find nourishment, and rely on my gut to decipher between fear and love.

During my first season in the late fall in Wyoming, I experienced a fire that made me find courage in adversity. It was the time of year when the aspen trees were changing colors, bears were rushing to eat everything before the snow came, and the evenings were accented with elk bugles. We were staying in barracks in the hills when a call came in to report a fire close by. When our crew got the report, we jumped into the trucks with all of our gear, thinking we would be returning in a few hours.

We hiked for a few hours to get into the fire, and the grueling march wore out everyone before we even got to the fire. When we finally had the fire's smoke in sight, we were overwhelmed with what we saw before us. We had to find the courage to act in the face of adversity and overcome the overwhelming nature of the task before us. There was not an abundance of smoke, but the fire had found a squirrel cache of pine cone trimmings which are a firefighter's worst nightmare. (Beds of pinecone scraps can be a few feet deep and extremely difficult to extinguish.) We sized up the situation, ordered all of the supplies we needed, and got to work. Once we got into the job, we discovered that this squirrel cache was unlike anything we had seen before. The fire was about five acres large (about six football fields) and six feet deep because of the squirrel cache. To really paint this picture, most fire lines are dug down six to ten inches until mineral soil is reached, but in this particular case, we had to dig trenches six feet deep to contain the smoldering squirrel cache. The ash from this particular fire was so fine we were all coughing up black after the first day on the job.

Putting in the containment lines took almost a week, whereas most five-acre cases would have taken a day. When we started mopping up (extinguishing every single hotspot) the middle of the fire, I remember balancing on logs that crisscrossed deep ash pits—one slip into the pits would have guaranteed full-body burns. It was in those moments, with sweat beads saturated with ash dripping into my eyes, that I realized we were doing something that had more risk than reward. The stir-up from the middle ash pits was nothing like I have ever seen. The substance emitted was equivalent to moon dust and coated the inside of our lungs with every swing of our tools. Honestly, all the efforts of our firefighting tools accomplished nothing in those ash pits; nothing could touch the smouldering pockets but snowfall, and even that was questionable hope. This challenge was one of the first times I used my Heart-Fire skills because I felt my heart urging me to stop balancing on logs above ash pits, swinging tools, and accomplishing nothing.

This was also one of my first experiences with the kind of suffering that builds resilience and mental fitness. Coughing up black for two weeks after this assignment was a constant reminder of this. In the end, I found that in life we sometimes repeatedly try the same high-risk approach to solve a problem with no results. However, what creates the results we seek is finding flow and the perfect balance between challenge and skill. This is a state where results are achieved when your mind leaves the body, time is lost, and action is perfectly completed without intentional thought. Flow-state should be the guiding feeling of the Heart-Fire Skills. If you are not in a flow-state, you are not being appropriately challenged with perfect resistance. Perfect resistance is the balancing of fear versus love.

Courage is very often needed in times of adversity and deciphering helpful courage from true life-or-death danger is often communicated by your gut. This is how I used my Heart-Fire skills to get off the logs hanging over the ash pits. I knew in my gut that I couldn't continue on that same life-path. Sensing danger with your gut is a powerful way to stay alive on all levels of life! Once your gut does its job and the basics of staying alive are met, it is time to find nourishment for the physical, emotional, mental, and spiritual parts of your life. Obtaining the necessary components for growth and well-being is my definition for finding nourishment. Imagine if your physical, emotional, mental, and spiritual selves had a cup and you needed to fill those cups every day to spur growth and wellbeing. Communicating to others is essential in order to receive everything you need to fill your cups, and this is the foundation of leadership. This sense of leadership is what allows you to set boundaries and embrace what you need to succeed. We are all leaders in some way and acknowledging that *you* are a leader for yourself is called Internal Leadership.

I started to find my personal growth and well-being during the summer of my seventh season in fire when I was faced with becoming a leader in a very real way. At the time I had been qualified to supervise five to seven firefighters on two-week fire assignments for a few years. I then took a new position where I supervised five to seven firefighters every day on a crew that was tasked with cutting trees in extreme terrain. We were to prepare defined areas of the forest by cutting trees and performing broadcast burns to help rebuild the aspen tree population. Idaho has lost eighty percent of its aspen stands which lowers the biodiversity of the ecosystem and negatively affects the elk populations. As far as our occupation goes, this type of assignment is the most dangerous thing you can do in the mountains.

Each day, my crew and I went for a morning run and then loaded up the trucks with our chainsaws and fuel and hit the road. After a thirty-minute drive or more we arrived at the project site, ready to slay trees for the day. We cut trees for fifty hours every week and if there was a fire report, we traveled out as the specialized chainsaw crew—we were the tree-cutting experts, and everyone knew it!

That year we were tasked with a specific project that required a seven-mile hike in, so all of our big gear was transported in by pack mule and we camped on the project site for the week. Most days were filled with tree dodging, close calls, and afternoon weather reports. It got to the point that we all itched for a fire call just so we could be on any other mountain but that one. We camped out on this project for a month and only hiked out for the weekends toward the end of the summer. We had no real food and mostly dined on spam and instant potatoes. There was no cell service to be found, so all contact with loved ones had to wait.

It was in that summer that I discovered that finding nourishment for mind and body was important to finding balance in life. Having harmony in the mind and body is essential to finding flow-state and purpose in life. That summer, I found nourishment by tuning in to my heart, taking a break from chain-sawing, and simply listening to the birds and wind in the trees. This truly helped me to find balance again. I also let the crew stop all chain-sawing every noon-hour and we all hiked a nearby mountaintop to just enjoy our work environment. This simple routine brought balance to all of us. I also made it a point to take the time to listen to my body and acknowledge when I needed a break. That summer taught me that taking a moment to realign my vibration back to my original instructions is invaluable because nourishment is more than just food and water; nourishment is whatever fills the cup inside your heart. This cup can be filled by anything physical, emotional, mental, or spiritual. I learned that leading myself and finding nourishment helped my crew find growth and well-being on all levels. Becoming a leader takes courage through adversity and deep self-work that illuminates the path toward growth and well-being every day. Don't forget—we are all leaders in some way! Acknowledging that you are a leader is the way in which you will find nourishment through your Heart-Fire skills because you will have to lead yourself in order to express your needs to those around you. You have to fill your chainsaw with fuel before you can use it!

When you have honed the ability to sense danger and have found nourishment, it is time to adventure toward finding true fulfillment, purpose, or a soul contract. Sometimes, before you have a true understanding of the purpose behind your instincts, you can sense yourself being pulled in a direction and that is all you need to take action.

The best example of this came when I worked a fire on the Arizona Strip a few years ago. The helicopter crew I worked on was on an assignment in Cedar City, Utah and we were dispatched to a fire call on the border of Utah and Arizona. We flew down with the basic complement for initial attack fires. With two firefighters, a chainsaw, hand tools, and sixty pounds of personal gear per person to keep us alive for forty-eight hours, we were ready.

When our helicopter arrived overhead, we saw a grass fire no bigger than a few hundred acres spreading in all directions at a noticeably slow pace for mid-July on the Arizona Strip. We made a game plan in the air, quickly landed next to the fire and jumped out to get to work. We retrieved all of our gear and hauled it to the black (the charred area the fire had already burned), so it would be safe. It turned out that it was a good thing we were so expeditious with this because when we dropped our bags and looked back, the helispot we just came from was already engulfed in fire. It was at this point that we knew we were in for a hard fight. While we were unloading, Air Attack (a plane that circles high above fires and supervises air resource) ordered single engine air tankers for retardant drops and a few heavy helicopters. Shortly after we got boots on the ground, I had multiple air resources that were depending on me for guidance from the ground.

Since I was the initial Incident Commander (the firefighter in charge of everything on the fire) until local resources came on the scene, I used the air resources as I saw fit. We used the retardant to box in the fire and the heavy helicopters with thousand-gallon water drops to hit the most active part of the fire. The air resources had to refuel within the hour, and as is the case with every fire, as soon as the air resources were down, the wind kicked up. Our fire of a few hundred acres quickly grew to a thousand acres in mere minutes. This all happened while the local resources were driving in to assist, and all four fire trucks got flat tires from the surrounding lava rocks. That left two firefighters to combat a grass fire about a thousand acres in size. In situations like that there is not much you can do besides wait in the black for the winds to die down.

All firetrucks finally arrived hours later and the aircraft returned and gave it their all, but the winds were unrelenting and the fire screamed across the grass with the unfortunate assistance of the wind. When I transferred command to the local units, we had no anchor points, no line—nothing. We soon made a twenty-person crew with the engines and helitack and divided into two groups to start the fight. Ten of us went one way and the remaining crew went in the opposite direction. By this time it was night, the desert winds were slowly calming down, and the temperature was dropping back into the bearable nineties. Even with the environmental assistance, ten people to each flank of a fire that size didn't buy us anything, and it certainly didn't help when we ran out of water to fight the fire. We used our water bags with wands as flappers to swat the fire's edge in an attempt to put it out. However, it was no use; lines of fire waved over the giant mesa on which we were standing. We decided to call the operation as a loss around midnight and we made our way back to our helitack gear. Unfortunately, the fire had changed so much that we were at a total loss as to where we should start walking to find our gear. To make matters worse, we were running out of drinking water. As the leader of our flank's team, I closed my eyes, took a deep breath, and let my gut tell me which way to walk. I opened my eyes, picked a direction, and started walking.

With waves of fire all around us, we couldn't determine what was black (safe) or green (ready to burn) because of the darkness of the desert night. We relied on our sense of smell, paid attention to the dust under our feet, and trusted our gut to guide us to safely walk in the black. (A strong fire leader knows never to walk through any green to reach the other side of a fire—that would dangerously put the team in between fuel and fire.) By simply using my gut as guidance to walk to the black edge of the fire, we found our helitack gear within the hour. We made camp for the night, slept on the ground, and woke at first light. To our relief, the winds had died down, the fire was thankfully out, and we were retrieved that afternoon with the helicopter.

I have learned that when the feeling in my stomach is heavy, tense, tight, or unsettled, it is a clear indicator that I am off-track. Conversely, when the feeling in my gut is relaxed, at ease, and experiencing flow, it is a clear indicator that I am on the right track. Sensing danger and direction are closely related in this sense, as well—one direction is safety and ease, and the other direction is struggle and death. Using the gut to find the right direction is a powerful practice that can guide you through the most tumultuous circumstances—I know this because I have done it and I have never gotten lost on the fire-line. Outside of firefighting, I have also used this technique to find direction when lost in life.

To reinforce and give meaning to direction, you need purpose to propel you over "the gap". The gap is the void between where you are now and where you want to be. Knowing where you want to be—finding direction— is only half the battle. You must bridge the gap and walk with purpose in the right direction toward your highest potential. You can find purpose with your heart by asking deep questions while in silence with the Infinity-Fire. Purpose can also come to you during meditation, a dream, or in a time of tremendous suffering. (It can also be found in deep silence and I will walk you through that process later in this book.) To get yourself started on the journey to finding your purpose, simply ask, "Why am I here? Who am I? What am I? What am I supposed to be doing? How can I serve on Earth?" These questions can help you to drill down and get at the root of your purpose. Remember: your Heart-Fire skills are recognizing danger, finding nourishment, sensing direction, and feeling purpose.

My Heart-Fire skills were revealed to me through wildland firefighting. Before I integrated my Heart-Fire skills, I never listened to my heart and I lived a directionless life. This is what led me into a severe case of heart fire that turned my world upside down. (Heart fire is different than the Heart-Fire to which I have thus far been referring.) I was diagnosed with a heart fire ailment in traditional Chinese medicine, which means my kidneys were too weak to cool down my overheating heart and the heat from my heart burned out of control in my body. In essence, I had a wildfire burning freely inside my internal organs. Eventually, the heat went from my chest into my head and burned my brain. This caused anxiety, insomnia, dilated pupils, and other physical symptoms. My vibrational field was lowered, and a feeling of grotesque heaviness washed over me for months. *(What exactly is a vibration? A vibration is the frequency at which energy is moving. A vibration determines the density of the universe around you. Your heart is a vibrational organ and your emotions are the vibrations that determine the frequency of your heart field.)*

Because of my heart fire ailment, I became stuck in a negative feedback loop of low vibration—I attracted illness with my lower vibrations, and I had low vibrations because I was sick. Until I understood why the Infinity-Fire had stricken me with heart fire ailment, I was a directionless lost soul. When I finally realized that my wildland firefighting career was a long and winding path to finding a spiritual practice, my heart fire symptoms subsided. Through dismissiveness and suffering I learned the lesson (the hard way) that the Infinity-Fire wanted me to. This book will guide *you* with grace to the Infinity-

Fire as a result of the lessons that I have lived and learned. You can bypass dismissal and unnecessary suffering if you are dedicated to the Infinity-Fire.

Furthermore, the seeker of the Infinity-Fire will benefit from learning Heart-Fire skills because these skills will forge the Infinity-Fire Triangles (self-love, conviction, spiritual power) between the universal consciousness and the seeker. The triangle of self-love is nourishing your body with breath, water, food, exercise, sleep, deep love, and accountability. The triangle of conviction is finding confidence, clarity, and certainty within your own heart. The triangle of spiritual power is when you align yourself with your highest-self and the Infinity-Fire. When all three triangles of self-love, conviction, and spiritual power are aligned, the Infinity-Fire alliance is created. The Infinity-Fire Alliance is the realization that we humans have the same nature as the Infinity-Fire. We are all aligned to unconditional love and compassion at the deepest levels. The Infinity-Fire alliance connects you to your higher-self and a higher power. The higher-self is the expression of your highest potential in all aspects and all realms. The higher-self grants you access to ancient wisdom that no book or guru could ever explain, and this ancient wisdom aids you in manifesting the reality of your soul's contract by helping you embody unconditional love and compassion. *Awakened by Heart-Fire* guides seekers in finding their secret connection to the Infinity-Fire so they can access their ancient wisdom.

In this book, I share my story and the ways in which I found my Heart-Fire after my awakening experience in deep meditation. Telling my story was essential so that I could integrate everything that the Infinity-Fire has taught me, and this journey has helped me personally integrate my Infinity-Fire to improve my teaching abilities. I hope my story captivates you and motivates you to explore your higher consciousness.

In *Awakened by Heart-Fire*, you will journey through your Heart-Fire to find a new connection to the Infinity-Fire that will result in deep self-reflection that will precipitate self-mastery. By mastering how you react to your thoughts and feelings, you will be able to control your actions. Being in control of any state of being at any given moment will allow you to manifest the reality you want. The foundation of self-mastery is built by connecting with your Infinity-Fire and listening to your Heart-Fire. Get ready for the deepest ride into the core of your consciousness to own your higher-self and attain the "impossible".

PART ONE

The East—Remember Heart-Fire

CHAPTER ONE

Heart-Fire Basics

In *Awakened by Heart-Fire*, I will describe two separate definitions of heart fire that will be differentiated by capitalization and hyphenation, and lowercase text. For instance, "Heart-Fire" is my own phrase and definition, while "heart fire" is defined as an ailment in traditional Chinese medicine. I define and view Heart-Fire as the ability to use the electromagnetic field of the heart to deepen one's connection to one's higher-self and the Infinity-Fire. It is a flameless fire that supports the expansion of unconditional love and compassion.

First, it's important to understand that classical Chinese medicine is a modality that has been used for more than 4,000 years by acupuncturists and doctors. Classical Chinese medicine is rooted in the knowledge that the human body is interconnected by the mind, body, and spirit. In Chinese medicine theory, there are three branches of energy similar to the mind, body, and spirit. Qi is closest to the idea of electrical currents in the nervous system or blood flow, and it helps to animate the human body. Jing relates to DNA and is the essence of the body while regulating growth, development, and reproduction. Lastly, there is Shen—the piece of the supernatural that is inside all of us, similar to the soul.

In addition, the organs in the body are interrelated so when one is out of sync, the entire body is slowly thrown off its equilibrium. Every major organ is also correlated with an element and an emotion. For example, the heart is connected to fire, the spleen to earth, the lungs to metal, the kidneys to water, and the liver to wood. Every organ is also interconnected through energetic conduits known as the Twelve Primary Meridians which allow Qi to flow through the body and nourish the organs in a natural rhythm. The manifestation of the Infinity-Fire is coursing through every being, and the ancient Chinese referred to this arrangement as Shen. Shen is the body's life force and the spark that gives the human body a soul. When one element of this beautiful system is out of balance, the whole bodily process will not properly function. This is where acupuncture intervenes to balance the Qi in the body.[2] Once this is accomplished, classical Chinese medicine helps restore balance to the Jing and Shen through food, herbs, spiritual practice, and meditations.

Along with needle treatments, classical Chinese medicine uses food as medicine and spiritual practice as the basis for all healing. Furthermore, because each organ is tied to an emotion, emotions that are not honored or processed induce blocked and dysfunctional vital life force energy in the associated organs and meridians. This dysfunction leads to blockages of Qi in the internal organ system and slowly degrades the validity of the whole mechanism that is the human body. For instance, grief and depression are connected to the lungs and large intestine, fear is associated with the kidneys and bladder, worry is the emotion of the spleen and stomach, anger and frustration are related to the liver and gallbladder, and happiness and joy are correlated with the heart and small intestine.[3]

Personally, I held anger in my being for most of my life and this led to heat rising from my liver into my heart. My kidney function was also lowered due to fear and stress from wildland firefighting for so many years.[4] The combination of these two occurrences caused my entire body to heat and eventually it became an extremely painful ailment. Because my anger/liver dysfunction was sending heat to my heart and my kidneys' energy level was so low, my heart was unable to cool itself.[5] This perfect storm ignited a fire in my heart; a fire with a flame that consumes. From this, I experienced a low-grade fever that lasted for six months that brought with it mania, anxiety, insomnia, and slight psychosis. I eventually learned that this is the traditional definition of a heart fire diagnosis in classical Chinese medicine.

What I learned from my healing crisis is that spirit was trying to teach me something! Spirit was trying to tell me to go deep into the cause of my heart fire. When I decided to journey deep into myself, I discovered that the element of my spirit is fire. It turns out that I am connected to fire on a much deeper level than just through my career. After six months of acupuncture and emotional healing I learned that I am a master of fire on all levels. Spirit was telling me to harness my skills because I had a higher purpose beyond being a wildland firefighter. I realized that I am here to master my heart fire and turn it into a power that can be shared with the world—my Heart-Fire. (Remember, this Heart-Fire power is different than the traditional heart fire in Chinese medicine.) I discovered that Heart-Fire is a burning desire, a guided passion, and a gateway to your highest potential. It is the force that expands unconditional love and compassionate action in your life.

Connecting with your Heart-Fire allows you to see, hear, and feel your environment with the heart's electromagnetic field. You can use your heart to see as your heart helps you to stay on a compassionate path. The heart center is also a conduit for the higher-self to speak. Additionally, you can use your heart to sense if your path leads to light or darkness which is commonly known as using intuition. This is not to be confused with psychic abilities which are a specific and predictive knowing about a future event. Hearing your higher-self speak through the heart is the natural way of living and having the ability to sense others' emotions with the heart (aka having empathy) is more accessible when your heart center is open.

Empathy is a powerful ability, but it needs to be controlled. For instance, if you walk into a busy market and feel everything that is happening with the hundred people around you, you will lose your sense of self in the sea of humanity. When empaths have a difficult time controlling their ability to feel what others are feeling, they often times turn to substance abuse to "turn off" their power. The foundation of creating boundaries for empaths is knowing where *their* emotions stop, and others begin. It is essential to be able to decipher the difference between your own emotions and those around you, and the ways in which you can return to a centered state. Connecting with a higher power and processing emotions every day is the way to open the conduit to the higher-self, which in turn opens the door to abilities such as intuition and empathy. *(We will review this technique in depth in a later chapter.)*

Holding a high vibration in the heart allows you to manifest your wildest dreams because high vibrations force the laws of attraction to commence. But remember, Heart-Fire skills are not uniquely special—everyone possesses these abilities. All you have to do is pay attention to your heart so that you can hear it whisper ancient wisdoms. Heart-Fire skills require intention, practice, and an openness to the extraordinary experience that is being a whole human. Being a whole human is about openly connecting to the Earth and Spirit realms, and eventually integrating both worlds.

These skills are desired by a Chātra in order to see, hear, and feel their environment with their Heart-Fire; this is the natural way of living. It truly is a way of life that imbues unconditional love and compassion into every moment, and, interestingly, it is the way Native Americans identified medicinal plants on the landscape. Native Americans didn't experiment with deadly or medicinal plants, but rather, they used their inner vision to show them the plants with medicinal properties. They asked their Heart-Fire to guide them into plant medicine. This is obviously a superior case of Heart-Fire skills that demonstrates its powerful possibilities; however, I don't recommend you try it without extreme dedication and a native elder mentor.

Heart-Fire skills connect you with your higher-self and allow you to access knowledge through your heart center that would otherwise be impossible to understand. The connection to your higher-self illuminates your soul's contract—your dharma—and helps you reach total fulfillment. Dharma is a universal law that states that following your soul's purpose allows you to live a life of flow and ease free from chaos because you and the universe are aligned toward achieving a mission. Your soul's contract is an agreement you make with the Infinity-Fire before you are born. This is a well-documented occurrence in *Life Between Lives: Hypnotherapy for Spiritual Regression* by Michael Newton.[6] In Michael Newton's work as a hypnotherapist, he found through thousands of past life regressions that his patients would convene with a council of spiritual beings between their lives. Thousands of patients recalled similar experiences in the life between lives describing a time where they got to select every aspect of their next life and then sign a contract before reincarnating. In other words, your soul's contract is your soul's purpose; it's what you need to be doing in this life in order to transfer learned lessons into the next and higher realm. Following your soul's purpose is in accordance with living your dharma. This includes living out actions with a sense of duty that are in harmony with nature, society, and the individual soul. Dharma is a cosmic law that propels all action, and when the cosmic law of life is being lived from unconditional love and compassion, the soul will be fulfilled.

Heart-Fire skills give you confidence in the wilderness of life as you navigate your spiritual path. You will know how to make solid life decisions free from doubt because the path of the heart never fails. Truly knowing that the heart never fails you is the foundation of conviction. When a Chātra has a soul-purpose and a driving conviction to that purpose, their life will radically change. When a driving purpose is grounded in unconditional love and compassion, that purpose will only produce miracles in all possible levels of life. While this all sounds wonderful, it doesn't mean that being guided by your Heart-Fire is not occasionally a messy and confusing process. Following my Heart-Fire was chaotic but through this chaos I developed a conviction to my Heart-Fire, and now I know it doesn't have to be chaotic. *You* can have grace and ease because I have forged the path forward by doing everything backwards for you. In the end, your heart knows how to find flow. Remember, flow is a state of awareness that arises when carrying out a task that falls between challenging and easy, where the body takes over all action. When this happens, time and thinking disappear. Living in flow is a path fostered by a divine agency and when followed, extraordinary spiritual growth will occur.

There is clearly room for error when we believe we are hearing our heart, but we must remember that it is our mind doing the speaking. The mind can be the trickster that makes you question everything at the last minute, confusing you as to whether or not you are on the right path. When I was on a fire assignment in the Boise area, I was training to be certified as an Engine Boss (a Captain in charge of a firetruck and crew). We were busy with initial attack fires every few days and the one I am going to tell you about was just another call; or so we thought.

We received the dispatch late in the evening, so darkness was due to fall in a few hours. This was "ops normal"—a slang term for "everything going as planned". I drove the twenty-four-thousand-pound truck and crew up the winding highway outside of Idaho City, Idaho toward the smoke that had initiated the call. We turned down a dusty dirt road a few miles from town and followed the dust trail behind the hotshots (elite wildland firefighting crew) on our way in. The first person to have arrived on scene ordered aircraft support, and by the size of the order, we knew we were going to be staying the night.

Of course, the hotshots beat us up the road—we were in a large, type-four engine about twenty-one feet in length and fifteen feet tall with seven hundred and fifty gallons of water on board. We finally got to the hotshot buggies (big troop carrier trucks), parked the engine, and watched the airshow while waiting for our instructions from the IC (Incident Commander). Our instructions came over the radio and the IC wanted our crew to hike in to add support to the hotshots. From my point of view, it looked like the hike would take a few hours, but it was getting dark and the fire activity was quickly increasing to the point of becoming unpredictable. So, as the leader-in-training, I made the call to leave the engine with the qualified Engine Boss, and I hiked in to scout out the fire before I sent my crew in.

If you have ever been to the Boise National Forest, you will know that it is steep—so steep in places that you need ropes to safely climb. So, I made the solo trek into the fire by following the noise of the helicopters and air tankers. My mind was saying, "Yes, you need to get to the fire tonight to prove that you are an Engine Boss!" However, my instincts were telling me that I was putting myself in a lot of danger. The hike took a few hours and I arrived at the fire by nightfall. (I actually remember running up the mountain when I heard the chainsaws of the hotshots.) I was thankful that I arrived when I did, because as soon as I met up with the hotshot supervisor, the fire took off roaring down the hill from which I had just hiked. There were snags (dead trees) dropping all around us, and we had nowhere to go but the black. I decided it wasn't safe for my crew to hike into the fire that night, so I called them off.

I spent the night on the mountain with the hotshots, fruitlessly digging line all night just to stay warm. The squad of hotshots (five to seven firefighters) and I dodged trees and were chased in circles by the fire. Because of my decision to do this alone, I left my crew behind, put myself in serious danger. I made it back to my crew the next morning, and because my work with the hotshots had altered my hours, I slept that day while my crew worked. Because I followed my mind the night before, driven by the need to prove that I could be an Engine Boss, I learned a powerful lesson. (I always learned more from my mistakes in fire than I did from my successes!) That experience taught me that when you're focused on what other people think of you instead of what is truly important, you become lost. I thought hiking into the fire alone would prove that I was tough enough to be an engine boss. I now know being tough has nothing to do with true leadership. My experience in Boise is an example of the mind's capability to manufacture dangerous scenarios. I never put myself at risk on the fireline when I followed my gut and listened to my heart, and this is why utilizing the power of discernment in the beginning of the decision-making process is critical. Always remember that the mind often gets us in trouble while the heart fills our paths with love. Heart-Fire shows you what you need to do, and your gut will tell you how to do it.

CHAPTER TWO

Wildland Firefighting with My Gut

Wildland firefighting is akin to an extreme sport, except we don't use skis or skateboards. Wildland firefighters ride waves of adrenaline with chainsaws, drip torches (canisters filled with a diesel and gas mix with a swirled tube and wick for lighting fires), and helicopters. We are tactical athletes that train for maximum endurance. We fall burning trees and light back-burns to save entire subdivisions. It is about as intense as civilian life gets and we face its inherent dangers every day.

Wildland firefighting teams typically consist of three to five people and firetrucks with water tanks. They can also be comprised of a twenty-person hotshot crew of highly experienced elite fitness fanatics groomed for the most extreme mountainous terrain and the most grueling wildland fire assignments imaginable. Helicopter crews are also specialized to fly two people into backcountry fires so they can do their work and hike out of the wilderness three to four days later. You may ask, "Why are these men and women risking their lives to save burning trees?" Sometimes these fires blow through whole stands of timber and march their way into the world of civilization, threatening housing developments, powerlines, dam infrastructure, and pipelines. These men and women are truly serving their country, not with assault rifles and Humvees, but with chainsaws, true grit, and resilience.

Late in my first season of fire, I physically and mentally had the hardest day of my life. It was late August and it had already been a busy fire season, but we were in the midst of a couple of slow days, so my crew and I were doing project work. We completed a six-mile run in the morning on a logging road through the mountains. We then returned back to the station and prepared our tree-cutting equipment before heading out to cut trees at the project site for the day. We used chainsaws to cut trees in order to reduce hazardous fuel build up around a subdivision of homes, and these trees were then chopped up into smaller pieces to burn in the winter months.

After a long day of cutting, we put all of the equipment back in the trucks and loaded up to go home for the weekend. At that moment, we received a fire call and all of our relieved and excited moods changed to a calming nervousness that every firefighter feels upon dispatch. The fire was burning near our station, and as we drove toward our houses, we could see a giant column of smoke behind the station, extending to the sky in the mountains. The sheer amount of smoke told us that we going to be stationed at that fire for a few weeks. The entire crew was so exhausted by this point since we ran six miles that morning and thinned trees and piled wood all day. Just to add to our exhaustion, the fire was burning at an oxygen-depleting elevation of ten-thousand feet.

When we showed up for our briefing, all I could stare at was the background fire as it consumed whole groups of trees and blew spot fires all over the mountains. Our crew was paired up with nine smoke jumpers to comprise a crew of seventeen people. We were to be the initial crew on scene, and not only were we exhausted, but we now had to keep up with the jumpers—the most elite human beings in the fire world. (There is no whining or slowing down around a jumper, because they are always tougher and more intense!)

It was only my second season and I wasn't allowed to chainsaw on fires yet, so I pulled brush for my sawyer as he cut down trees out of the way of the fire. I was so tired that I wanted to collapse as I started to pull my first pieces of tree and brush. I wanted to go home to my bed hours ago, but there was no rest for the weary. (It's at points like this that wildland firefighters find internal strength. It isn't a physical but rather a mental toughness that creates resiliency the harder a mission gets.) I pushed my body as far as I could, but we were surrounded by fire and were losing our fight. When you are that exhausted and have worked for over sixteen hours, the crew's morale starts to falter, and serious mistakes can occur. (Firefighters often use chewing tobacco to keep up their morale, and to keep from slipping into mental confusion. It's like a trigger—every chew gives them a boost of mental confidence that pulls them through the most extreme situations.)

Resilience is the ability to create opportunity out of any adversity and to flourish in the suffering of a situation. Borrowed from the military, a slang phrase you often hear on the fireline is, "embrace the suck". Resilience is equivalent to mental fitness and is the way in which you react to the most extreme stress in the mind and body. Mental fitness is the way in which you come back from intense struggle, regroup, and conquer said struggle with a positive attitude.

So, we continued the mental beatings of fighting the fire until our morale improved. We did this until we were so exhausted that we became silly, flamboyant, and lost sight of the seriousness of the situation. We cut trees in an attempt to slow down the fire until one in the morning. When all was said and done, we worked a seventeen-hour shift that day. When it was time for sleep, we bedded down in a meadow, huddled together in an attempt to stay warm and discourage any bear attacks.

In the morning, we saw that the fire hadn't taken any breaks during the night, and all of the work we had done was lost. As is often the case, just when you think you have a good line around a fire, you don't. When this happens, it compounds the need for resilience because you cannot get frustrated when your work gets burned over; it's the nature of fire to burn anywhere it possibly can. (Without question, if you leave any opening for fire to exploit, it will!) We stayed on this particular fire for two weeks and it eventually burned over an entire camp of five hundred people, but that is a story for later. (Disclaimer: no one was hurt!)

These types of forest fires are typically started from lightning in the mountains during a summer dry spell, or from someone having a bonfire in the suburbs on a windy day. Rarely, and most unfortunately, these sprawling forest fires are ignited from pre-meditated arson. However they are started, wildland fires burn in various conditions and with various fuel types including grass, timber, and brush. For instance, wildland fires have started in the mountains of the Northern Rockies when the pine needle groundcover has dried to weightless tinder dust in the dry fall air. Once fires such as these become established, all bets are off because with one good wind, they can destroy entire drainage systems and mountainsides. There is nothing humans can do except strategically light more fire to try and stop it, because it is impossible to predict these behemoths once they stand up and roar.

In other areas of the country like Nevada, the sea of cheatgrass allows fire to flow across the landscape for miles at a time, hitching a ride on a windy day. Cheatgrass is an invasive species from Europe, southwestern Asia, and northern Africa that loves fire—the more it burns, the more it spreads its seeds. A cheatgrass fire in high wind can easily travel twenty or thirty miles in a day. Nothing will stop it except for a strategic burn off of a road about a mile ahead of the flame-front. (Not only is cheatgrass a friend to fire, it is also killing the local sage population and making Nevada a sterilized state with a monoculture of foreign grass that is lowering biodiversity. It has become a nightmare for natural resource managers.)

I remember one particular fire call that came when I was in Texas for a few months during the spring. I was on the same type four engine as previously mentioned, and it was equipped with seven hundred and fifty gallons of water on board. I also had six firefighters with me that were itching to crush the next blaze. We received a dispatch outside of Lubbock, Texas, and the reported fire was close—it was about thirty miles from our assigned station, freely burning along the major freeway. We threw on the lights and sirens and drove with speedy caution toward the report. By the time we arrived on the scene about thirty minutes later, the fire had run nineteen miles up the highway and extinguished. This is the essence of cheat grass fires—they catch the wind and run. When the wind stops, the fire stops. As firefighters, we don't really fight this kind of fire unless we need to burn off roads miles and miles ahead of a running fire.

The Boise front range have faced severe fires for the past ten years. Entire mountain ranges and deep drainages will never regrow the lost timber due to soil sterilization, and the only thing that can flourish on the landscape is sage brush. The Boise front range is unfortunately the best example of desertification and irreversible landscape alteration as the result of extreme fires—for the next 500 years, at least.

Whenever we go to the Boise front, we know to keep our heads on a swivel because of the unpredictable nature of the landscape. Ponderosa pine, grass, and sagebrush mix with extreme temperatures to create explosive burning conditions. I remember watching a desert fire outside of Boise grow to over a million acres in a few days, leaving nothing but slicked-off black—the resulting smooth and sterilized ground after a fire burns through with extreme intensity.

No matter how or why a fire has started, when the fire-call comes in, the specialized wildland fire teams are ordered through a dispatch center and relayed coordinates. The rookies at the station are drooling with excitement to get out there and get broken in, while the old-timers are happy just to put in another day and inch closer to retirement. Regardless, the mission is simple: put out fires when the fire conditions are severe because there are consequences. When the engine crews and hotshot crews are not on fires, they are out in the woods cutting trees and making the landscape safer one sapling at a time. No matter what time of year or what part of the country you're in, there is a wildland firefighter somewhere training for fire season or hiking through blood, sweat, and tears to save a forest. Even in the off-season, they're readying their minds and bodies for the upcoming season of inevitable fires.

Consequently, the dangers of being on the frontlines are no joke. Between ghostly trees falling without warning, unimaginable mountainous roads that should not be traversed—let alone with a giant firetruck—the possibility of helicopter crashes, rolling rocks and logs, and the constant threat of being trapped in a burn-zone, the frontlines are fraught with perilous danger. I can't count how many times I have seen burned up trees fall without warning. One time, a ghost tree fell right in front of me and struck another firefighter, dropping him to his knees. Luckily, the tree landed on a stump before it hit the firefighter, otherwise it would have crushed him to death. We moved the tree, made sure he was fine to continue on, and laughed our way up the fireline. After so many years on the job, it's normal to witness close calls and then shrug them off out of necessity. After a couple of uneventful fires, we become numb to the stress and danger around us, and we have the tendency to let down our guard. Normalization of danger leads wildland fire teams to become complacent and complacency is always the first indication of a pending accident. All it takes is someone getting hurt to snap us out of that fog, and we immediately return to the feeling that everything is going to kill us if we don't listen to our guts. *(Getting trapped in a burn-zone is always in the back of a wildland firefighter's mind and it is the worst-case scenario because if it happens, it indicates that you broke some sort of standard order; you broke the code of safety as the first priority. This negatively impacts the trust and respect that the fire community has for you, and there is no going back.)*

Infamous incidents like Storm King, Yarnell, and Mann Gulch make the whole wildland fire community stop and think about what they are doing out there. These famous fires are examples of entire crews getting caught in a burn zone with tragic consequences. (God rest the souls of the fallen, and we thank you for all of your sacrifices every time one of us jumps from a plane, repels from a helicopter, or steps out of a truck.) We all carry these events in our minds because we train to the bad outcomes and the ways in which we can avoid repeating them.

Generations of wildland firefighters have synthesized all of the tragedy fires into Common Denominators that we all watch out for on the line. The Common Denominators are:

- Most incidents happen on smaller fires or on isolated portions of larger fires.

- Most fires are innocent in appearance before unexpected shifts in wind direction and/or speed result in flare-ups or extreme fire behavior. In some cases, tragedies occur in the mop-up stage. (This can happen when a fire appears extinguished but is still burning deep in the ground.)

- Flare-ups generally occur in deceptively light fuels, such as grass and light brush.

- Fires run uphill surprisingly fast in chimneys, saddles, gullies, and on steep slopes. (These are specific terrain features.)

- Some suppression tools such as helicopters or air tankers can adversely affect fire behavior. The blasts of air from low-flying helicopters and air tankers have been known to cause flare-ups.[7]

(I encourage you to find the metaphor in the common denominators and find your own common denominators for life so you can be on alert for what compromises your health, safety, and happiness.)

This is where wildland firefighting intersects with the gut; every great firefighter is in tune with their gut because they have to be. The gut can be trained to scream when a possible common denominator is present. *How else can anyone know with certainty what a fire will do in the hot, dry afternoon?* There are too many variables in wildland fires including fuels, weather, topography, and past fire history, so I learned to always go with my gut in field operations. Every briefing I ever attended ended with "fight fire with your gut", and I used my gut in every high-risk situation to hone my skills in the field. Because of this, I stayed alive and became a gut master.

I was once the Incident Commander of a fire (the person responsible for everything on a fire mission) and I made the call for all forces to immediately retreat. There was only one road to take out of the fire, and it was bad, slow, and unforgiving. I called all thirty firefighters off the fire and ordered them to drive miles and miles down the road to safety. Within an hour, the fire had completely blown up and burned across the road that we had just retreated down. I called off all operations except for air attacks, because I knew in my gut that a bad outcome waited for us on that mountain. I was so glad I listened to my gut.

Why does listening to your gut work in high-risk situations when there are too many variables to logically process? How did I instantly make decisions and feel comfortable with them? I used my gut because I know that the gut is in tune with an unseen force that allows the body to gather data without seeing, hearing, or feeling. This unseen force is spirit or universal consciousness. The gut and heart are the seat of psychic powers/inner vision/intuition—whatever you want to call it! The heart can tell you what you *need* to be doing, but your gut will tell you *how* to get it done.

After years of fighting fire with my gut, I could look at a landscape, check the weather, and understand the probabilities of which drainages were going to burn today, tomorrow, or in a week. I was always able to tell the general direction of the fire and place a reliable bet on where we would be fighting the next day, even when the fire did something unexpected.

Furthermore, I always used my gut to evaluate hazard trees before I put the chainsaw to them. Whenever I was out ahead of my crew, scouting where to place the fireline in relation to where and how fast the fire was burning, I consulted my gut. If I was driving through a subdivision in a firetruck triaging buildings and creating a structure plan, I had to know whether or not a house was defensible. I asked my gut which houses I would spend time on, and which ones were not worth the risk.

One season, I was leading a twenty-person hand crew in Chelan, WA and the operational plan was to put fireline from the rock fields in the mountains all the way down to the lake. The operation was about nine miles long, and after the heavy equipment including bulldozers opened up easy fireline and our hand crew was plugged in to fortify the nine miles of dozer line from top to bottom, we got to work and I started to scout out the project including the demarcation of our safety zone at the lake. (A safety zone is somewhere a firefighter is so safe they could take a nap.) I wanted to check out our safe place and time our escape route so I would know my crew would be safe in the worst-case scenarios. After scouting, I was horrified to discover that none of the upper management had done any scouting before me. When I got to the lake, I discovered that there was a 200-foot cliff with no way down to the lake. This was a no-go. We didn't have a safety zone. Operational planning at the higher level was flawed and we were in the position of breaking the code that stated we needed to make safety our top priority.

Once I realized this, my gut started to turn, I felt heavy, everything slowed down, and my entire body tensed; I knew we were all in a bad situation. My gut told me that we shouldn't be there. It was then that I remembered one of my crewmembers in the back seat on the drive in saying, "This drainage feels like one of the posters you see at the station of the fatality fires." I agreed and rallied all of the crew bosses on the division to deny the operational plan due to it being unsound. I painted a picture of the fire for the upper management showing them that our needs were not being met at the ground level. We didn't have a safety zone and that was a no go on my checklist as a Crew Boss. I took it upon myself to lead up and ask for the group's needs to be met before we engaged in firefighting.

The Crew Bosses and hotshot supervisors eventually devised a better plan with the Operations Section Chief and Division Supervisors to mitigate the extreme risk. We still put in the fireline, but my team and I thoroughly talked it out beforehand to weigh the risks and rewards. In the end, the complete plan never reached its end-state.

The Operations Section Chief wanted us to burn out the line, but there was a mutiny from the crews on the ground level due to a lack of safety zones.

During the summer of 2016, I obtained my Engine Boss qualification which meant that I was able to run an entire fire engine crew by myself. The following week, my engine captain was off, and it was my turn to run the module. We were called up to a fire in Grand Teton National Park and the southern border of Yellowstone National Park. We were prepping buildings (getting them ready for a flame-front) at the south entrance of Yellowstone, with the assumption that we had a few days before the fire came. We were in the midst of organizing a cache of hoses and fittings for the sprinkler systems we were going to install around the development and, as the Engine Boss, I was tuned in to Air Attack (the plane that circles a fire to report findings to the Incident Commander [IC] and ground resources). I heard the plane relay to the IC that the fire was a few days out but increasing in speed. The flame lengths were 200 feet high and they were slowly chewing around a lake a few miles from our position.

A few minutes later, I heard Air Attack on the radio screaming, "Get all ground resources out of there now! If there is anyone at the south entrance of Yellowstone, get out now!" The fire hadn't just picked up in speed, it had suddenly run a mile through heavy timber in about thirty minutes. We all jumped into the fire engine, turned the lights on, and sped down the highway. Our safety zone was just down the road and I had the pedal to the floor the entire time. As the leader of the module, I was terrified for the safety of my crew. My mind was racing—my heart knew we would make it, but I was truly questioning how it would unfold. The fire had already crossed the highway between us and our safety zone, but I was hoping we could make it through. When we arrived at the fire zone, the fire was on both sides of the road and we lost the highway for a minute in the heavy smoke.

My heart sank with uncertainty and my mind raced so fast that time slowed down as we watched fire on both sides of the road. It was as if we could almost hear every flicker of flame around us. I could hear crew members sweating in the silence of despair we were all experiencing. I had to swerve to dodge falling trees and the cab of the truck started to get warmer as the fire closed in outside our windows. Luckily, our safety zone wasn't far, and just as we crossed into the flame front, we passed through. I wonder if we all held our breath at some point because when we came out of the smoke and saw the turn to our safe place, we all let out a huge collective sigh, and we quickly returned to our jovial nature. (Every firefighter flourishes when the fire is hot; it's born of the feeling that this is what they're destined to do here on Earth. The adrenaline that invariably accompanies every fire becomes a way of life and makes a wildland firefighter feel alive.)

When we pulled into our safety zone, a 300-foot flame front slammed the control lines around us. Within a minute, we were completely surrounded by 300-foot flames, but we were safe in the middle of a parking lot. The sky dimmed black with smoke and the heat penetrated the cab of the engine. Our Division Supervisor handed out his resources-instructions to save as many surrounding structures as possible. When we were able to exit the truck, we made our rounds between pulses of fire and put out little spot-fires between cabins, houses, and a nearby lodge. At least fifteen pulses of fire came through that night and we were bombarded by 300-foot flames until about three in the morning. We slept in a gravel parking lot for about two or three hours before the sun came up and relief forces arrived to assess the damage. This was my first qualified Engine Boss assignment and damn—that was a crazy night of fire.

There is an unexpected bridge between wildland fire and intuition. Being a wildland firefighter is like going to an academy for intuition and living by your gut. The most profound skill I learned in my fire career was to use my gut to sense danger, morale levels, emotional torment, and poor leadership. This mastery of the gut helped me build my intuition and connect to my heart's field of vision. When I learned to listen to my heart, follow my gut, and use my brain, I became a powerful leader in wildland fire.

What's gratifying to hear is that this connection of gut, heart, and brain is now being proven in science. Though perhaps a little surprising, there are more neural connections in the gut and heart than in the brain.[8] Using the entire nervous system to see, hear, and feel your environment seems like an unorthodox approach to life, yet this is the basis for Heart-Fire skills and is exactly what I learned to do while fighting wildland fires. The entire nervous system seems to operate as one in the state of flow. (Remember: Flow is when you are so focused on a task that you lose sense of time and all awareness of your body. There has to be a perfect balance between skill and challenge for flow to manifest.)

For me, flow in life-or-death situations is where I connected with my true potential. Cutting nasty burned trees always brought me into a flow state, but the most dangerous situations always doubled my productivity. I remember driving a heavy firetruck that weighed about twenty-four thousand pounds filled with water, gear, and a full crew up a mountain road in the middle of a desolate part of Wyoming. Air Attack called in a fire on the radio as my backseat firefighters searched in all directions for signs of smoke. The non-stop radio chatter was only interrupted by the laughs of my crew as they enjoyed the ride. I, however, drove down a road that was so terrifying I had to drop into flow-state to keep everyone safe. (The feeling of flow-state is best described as a hyper focused mindset that still allows you to see everything in your peripheral vision. You hear everything at once, but you have an enhanced ability to pick out the important information. Time seems to not exist because it is just you and your task.)

I distinctly remember driving this road with a heavy truck full of firefighters, all the while knowing that everyone's life was in my hands—one small mistake and the truck could leave the dirt road and careen down a thousand-foot embankment. I had to take in every possible factor and manage micro-adjustments that only professional drivers could notice. With only a few inches of shoulder between safety and probable death, driving forest roads in a heavy engine is one of the most dangerous things a wildland firefighter will ever do. Driving kills more fire men and women than anything we do, so I used flow-state to simultaneously harness my gut, heart, and brain power to keep my crew safe.

We rely on flow-state every single day to stay alive, and this is how wildland firefighters become masters of flow. We tend to get so deeply involved in a task that time seems to stop, and it makes it seem as if there is nothing in the world but us and our drip torches on the side of a mountain. Wildland firefighting is where I honed flow-state, found my gut, and field-tested it over and over again. Remember: the heart will always tell you what you need to be doing and the gut will tell you how to do it.

CHAPTER THREE

Awakened by Heart-Fire

I stumbled onto my awakening experience without the proper preparation, and for that I paid dearly for my instant access to the Infinity-Fire. My goal in this book is to show you how to prepare your mind, body, and spirit before you experience an awakening event. This book is designed to help you walk down your spiritual path with grace and purpose. From experience, don't force a kundalini awakening (described in ancient yogic texts as an instant vision experience of the entirety of the universe while experiencing all of time in a single moment) like I did, as it took almost a year of acupuncture to re-stabilize my body. This is my story from this unprepared and earth-shattering awakening:

In 2017, my gut told me to start meditating more and to practice yoga and qigong. Once I formed this daily habit, I started to enjoy the benefits of my practice. I went deep into meditations, journaled, and practiced yoga and qigong for two hours every day. My spirit was exploding with freedom and I became addicted to the connection I felt with the divine.

One time, during a late-night meditation session, I was practicing an ancient qigong method that circulated Qi through the body. I began to truly feel the energy moving in my body and I discovered that I could control it. This was a major breakthrough for me, and I became obsessed with focusing on my Qi. Near the end of my meditation that night, I asked spirit to unlock my third eye. I said out loud, "Please unlock my third eye so I can see the universe." I felt an electric shock at the base of my spine shoot like a rocket all the way up my back and out of my head.

What happened next was unbelievable and my former reality was burned away in an instant. I was suddenly thrown out of my body and into space above the Earth. I was confused and I wondered if I had died. In this newfound form of astral projection, I was free—I was looking at the Earth as a whole. I understood the feeling that astronauts always speak about, because seeing the Earth as one biosphere changed everything.

In my new state of awareness, I noticed the sun and felt attracted to the light. Like a moth to the flame, I was drawn toward the sun and I made a conscious effort to float toward our star. As I got closer and closer, I was pulled into the center of the sun by a deep curiosity. To my surprise, the sun was a portal that connected to the next closest sun. I followed the sun trails to the next star and the next sun. I flew from one star to the next like the starship USS Enterprise, hopping from star to star and solar system to solar system. There was a light trail that connected all the suns in the entire galaxy, and I followed the most direct path to the center of the galaxy, driven by an unquenchable curiosity. When I arrived at the center of the Milky Way, I was in shock to see the center of the galaxy. The beauty was awe-inspiring and indescribable. The sheer gravity tore my body apart and I was drawn into the black hole.

My soul shards then traveled into the super massive black hole in the center of our galaxy. On the other side of the hole, there were light paths connecting to the next closest black holes. This was a fractal of the light paths that existed between stars and galaxies. (A fractal is a geometric pattern that repeats on all scales.) I followed the portals of black holes through all of the galaxies on my way to the center of the universe. When I got to the center of the universe, I lost all form and the black holes disappeared. I began to zoom out and zoom out, and I zoomed out so far out that I could see the entire universe as one whole—another fractal of seeing the Earth as one biosphere.

It was dazzling to see galaxy clusters connected to galaxy clusters by light paths, confirming that the universe is made up of geometric mathematical fractals. Then I noticed a sparking in one section of the web of light. Sparks flew and then traveled to be sparked again, instantly flying across vast amounts of space. Then it hit me: I was looking at the brain of the universe. The universe is a super massive neural network of super consciousness. After I was given this answer to the most universal question, I was thrust back into my body and I was never the same person.

When I came-to the next morning, I was in a world I didn't recognize, and my heart was whispering to me. I heard my heart for the first time, and it told me that I was on a mission to help people. However, my body was hot and unfamiliar, and I felt a fire inside my head and chest that was making me uncomfortable. I had a burning sensation on the exact point of my third eye that wouldn't dissipate—it was a constant burning that lasted for months! The fire had traveled from my chest area to my head and I was completely disarmed by it. As a result, I suffered from deep anxiety, insomnia, and mania for a few months.

I started to feel like I was going crazy because I couldn't stop myself from performing the ancient Chinese technique of moving my Qi, and I became stuck in a pattern and in loops of thought. My heat was intensifying, and I developed anxiety. The fire in my chest traveled to my head and I felt burning in my brain from over-activity. I looked in the mirror, saw my dilated pupils, and felt my anxiety increase. I saw geometric patterns during the day, thought I was going to die any second, and I was constantly sweating from a fever. As a result, I didn't sleep for a few months and I started to suffer from deep and uncontrollable anxiety. (In classical Chinese medicine, my heart fire was out of balance and my kidney water was too low to cool down my heart.) I slowly died alive over the ensuing year, experiencing what the Native Americans call a "shamanic death". I lost all ties to my old self, and my mind, body, and spirit started to rearrange into a new Thomas.

From experience, **do not** force a kundalini awakening like I did. It took six to twelve months of acupuncture to stabilize my body. This is why protection and grounding yourself every day is so essential. Focus your energy back toward your lower Dan Tian, and your feet will save you from the experience I endured. (Your lower Dan Tian is your center of gravity just below the navel and it is where your life force originates in Chinese medicine. Always bring any meditation back to your lower Dan Tian.) I will teach you a protection and grounding meditation in a later chapter that is the foundation of the Heart-Fire method.

CHAPTER FOUR

Fire Inside Me

From a very young age I have always had an affinity for fire—it even got me in trouble as a child. When I was about five years old, my father traveled for weeks at a time for work. As a souvenir of his travels, my dad brought home a matchbook from the hotels at which he stayed and collected them in a large bowl on our living room bookcase. One summer day, my friend and I were terribly bored when we spotted that bowl of matches. We took it outside and started lighting the matches one at a time. We did that until it became boring, and then we moved to lighting a campfire in the backyard woods. We did that until it got boring, and then we lit even more campfires. The next thing we knew, my backyard was crackling with seven campfires and we were out of matches. My mother luckily arrived at that point and we were in *so* much trouble! I will never forget the scolding we received and the guilt that I felt from burning my dad's priceless collection of matchbooks. That bowl of matches was a sentimental passport of his travels, and I only recently forgave myself for what I did that day.

As much as that experience negatively impacted me, I still had the desire to see what fire could be like at its most extreme. This ultimately became my driving factor for becoming a wildland firefighter, because it afforded me the opportunity to explore and harness my attraction to fire while also helping others. Even now, when I watch fire, it fills me with peace and brings me closer to deeper understandings of the universe. Fire is the universal cleanser and recycler of paths, consuming everything in its way while replenishing the soil of essential minerals. Fire takes hundreds of years of forest succession—the occurrence of old growth trees turning into nurse logs (old and rotted logs on the forest floor that miraculously sprout saplings form their carcasses)—and accelerates the process into mere years.

On a personal level, fire also reminds me that I used to live in pure anger because fire is the color of frustration and I would see its reddish hues when I was angry. Wildland firefighting allowed me to let out my rage when I chainsawed everything in my vicinity, and my rage allowed me to put in faster and better saw lines than anyone around me. Fire allowed me to go into "beast mode" and use my anger toward a productive end-goal. (Beast mode is similar to flow-state, but the driving factor is rage and anger. It is like turning on a hose of anger that fuels imperfect action while achieving results when channeled through something like chainsawing, firefighting, working out, etc.)

Wildland firefighting is the passion that allowed me to express my anger to maximum capacity without any judgement from others. I could be angry, and my fellow brethren fed off my "get-it-done-anger" attitude. I used anger to get up mountains, to hike fifteen miles to the nearest road, and to take down trees while saving others. Wildland firefighting did more than let out my rage and get me up the mountain; I found my Heart-Fire skills out there on the fireline and learned how to transmute my anger into peace and unconditional love. My Heart-Fire—the fire that doesn't burn but supports life—didn't transfer my anger like wildland firefighting, but rather, it transmuted my anger into love. *This is the secret to real anger management.* (I previously tried clinical therapy to address my anger and I only learned how to hide my anger even better. Hidden anger is a seed of illness and if germinated, it can flourish into violence.)

The universe speaks to me through fire because fire allowed me to connect to my higher-self and the Infinity-Fire. By studying fire on the landscape, I in turn studied myself and came into an awakening. I now have the ability to watch a fire flow across a ridge and know where it will be tomorrow through the wisdom of the Infinity-Fire. I have watched sleeping giants in the bottom of canyons and my Heart-Fire showed me where the fire would wake up and blow out the entire drainage. I have seen fire in all aspects of my life, and it became my mentor. I am a student of fire at the deepest levels; fire is my element and my healing agent of growth. I love my spiritual teacher, fire. Fire showed me how to rid my body of anger the hard way. After watching fire for so long, I shouldn't be surprised that it has taught me so much through abrupt and harsh lessons. I also learned that all fire is not created equal. Some fire has a flame that destroys and requires rebuilding, while other more ethereal fire is flameless. The latter is the foundation of life and supports the expansion of love.

During my wildland firefighting career, I realized that I could never let out enough anger even after I poured red-hot hate onto every fireline. If I had the power, I would have torn apart the entire world at that time. I thought I had dealt with my anger in every aspect, but in every battle with fire, I only depleted my anger for a short time. I used anger to hike, chainsaw, and endure grueling workouts. I used anger as motivation when the mission didn't make sense, but we were doing it anyway. There was no bottom to the source of my anger—it always came back like an insidious weed. No amount of burning, beating, running, or hating ever transformed my anger. So, in an effort to try something new, I attempted to suppress it. After years of expression, I tried to hide my anger. At first, I thought dismissing my frustrations was working because I didn't feel angry, but the anger was secretly building inside my liver, creating heat, and waiting for the right time to explode in a fireball from my liver, to my heart, and finally to my head. (In traditional Chinese medicine, anger is associated with the liver and it causes energy blockages that result in dysfunction.)

When my heart fire (Chinese medicine ailment) was out of balance, the only comfort I ever found was in trying to determine the lessons the Infinity-Fire gave me during my journey through anxiety. The way I learned to heal myself was to understand the lessons behind the suffering. *Was fire telling me to go deeper into my meditations to see the lessons I needed to learn? How was fire alluding to a shamanic rebirth? What was I so angry about?* A lesson was waiting to be unwrapped with every angry thought, and I learned to celebrate my anger because it illuminated learning opportunities and proved to me that my work wasn't done. Behind all of that anger, I also knew that I was scared. I had always been afraid of my anger because I knew it had the power to transform me into a beast. *(As a teenager, I once threw all the upstairs furniture in my house down the stairs. When I didn't land a skateboard trick, I would punch myself or break my skateboard out of rage.)*

I was always afraid of truly unleashing my anger because I worried that I might hurt someone, and I would never intentionally want to hurt another being because it goes against all of my values. This fear built up in my kidneys and weakened the water element in my body, lowering the ability of my kidneys to cool down my heart. My heart fire burned out of control with less water available to cool my heart. The fear and anger are what allowed the heat to pass through my heart, into my head, and to start burning my brain. This made my whole body overheat, and my skin felt like it was melting. I experienced mania, anxiety, and a low-grade fever for months on end.

I learned that my TCM heart fire diagnosis was telling me that the answer was in the fire itself. *Fire was the answer and Infinity-Fire was speaking, but was I listening?* The uncomfortable heat in my body and my low-grade fever were the answer to my spiritual quest. Over time, the low-grade fire in my body forced me to go deep into self-healing work, which helped me burn away all of my negative thoughts and emotions. The flameless fire (Infinity-Fire) healed me and like a new sprout of grass in a sea of ash, I was rebuilding. To be clear, this is not the proper energetic use of fire. I was ravaged by a fire inside my body and forced to do inner work, but I'm here to tell you that you don't have to be burned by fire to heal, grow, flourish, and change into anything you want. Learn from me and harness the power of the flameless fire; the Infinity-Fire.

I don't recommend replicating my exact personal journey because it was dangerous for my health and it was also very uncomfortable. When I understood what I was supposed to learn from having a fire inside me, I decided to integrate the fire into my soul. This helped me to learn that the fire was here to help me see my true nature and learning the purpose of the fire was enough for me to change vibrations. The intense self-work burned away my negative emotions and detoxified my heart. Fire forced me to deal with my emotions in the now because my life depended on it. I was truly going to die or go crazy if I didn't balance my heart fire. I know this because at my first acupuncture treatment, my doctor said, "Your anger is killing you." I will never forget that. That small sentence snapped me out of a trance, and I continued acupuncture and deep spiritual work for six months before the fire in my body subsided and anchored into balance.

When I finally balanced my heart fire in my body, I heard my heart speak to me for the first time. I then realized that I had been using my Heart-Fire to sense direction, danger, and nourishment for years. My Heart-Fire was all I needed to connect to my higher-self and the Infinity-Fire—I could see with my heart! Intentionally seeing with my heart for the first time made me feel a little insane. I thought, "This can't be real," but it was. Since that acceptance, my heart has never led me astray because I trust it and the more I trust it to spiritually guide me, the happier I feel. The more my Heart-Fire drives my life, the more personal power I gain. I mastered my heart fire by converting it into the solution. I identified a problem, learned from it, and made a solution by changing my position. *This is exactly how you fight wildland fires—you see a problem, you take advantage of any weakness it reveals, and you use it against itself.* It is also the same principled approach in martial arts or Taichi, namely the redirection of energy. In the midst of chaos, there is also opportunity.[9]

I do not recommend you try to have a fire inside yourself; it was a frightening experience and my health paid dearly for it. I fought the fire inside me so you could learn your Heart-Fire skills with grace. Playing with fire inside your body is dangerous, so I recommend that you *study* the flameless fire and find endless wisdom instead. In summation, I played with the wrong fire—the flaming fire—and now I am inviting you to study the flameless fire—the Infinity-Fire.

CHAPTER FIVE

Infinity-Fire Alliance

The Infinity-Fire is a level of super-consciousness that has an affinity for all beings of the universe. The Infinity-Fire bases all actions on the highest good for all which means using unconditional love and compassion for all actions. When you have aligned with your highest-self, Heart-Fire, and Infinity-Fire, you are reminded that the natural state of being is flowing with ease and following your heart. The Infinity-Fire Alliance occurs when an alignment is made between the three triangles of self-love, conviction, and spiritual power, and the Infinity-Fire. This must happen while also basing all actions on unconditional love and compassion, with consideration for the highest good for all. In your life, attuning your actions to the highest good for all is a tracking tool that lets you know how aligned you are with the Infinity-Fire.

To help explain this phenomenon, I want to tell you a story of my time on a holding team during a prescribed burn in Wyoming. (Holding teams keep the fire inside predetermined lines.) The lighters—firefighters with fire-carrying devices to light the forest on fire—were running strips of fire perpendicular to me and were walking from one containment line across the unit to another containment line. They waited for the fire to grow together and then executed another pass.

As I stood on the edge of the fire, I watched a single torch (the term for a tree that is fully engulfed in fire) and a voice inside me told me to pay close attention because an important lesson was about to unfold. The tree was completely overtaken by fire, and its raw and powerful beauty was beyond words. I watched as embers floated down from up high, propelled by the moving air generated from the hot thermals that torching typically creates. I was mesmerized as I watched an ember land a few feet away on the ground. I watched it fizzle, spark, and start a new fire. (Spotting is the technical term for new fires created by embers.) I had this realization that just as fuel, heat, and oxygen are required for fire to breathe, humans need the Infinity-Fire to spark a Heart-Fire inside of our bodies so we can breathe in life. I understood in an instant that the torching tree was the Infinity-Fire and the ember that sparked the spot fire was the Heart-Fire. In essence, this is the way life is energetically created in the universe—we all carry a spot fire in our hearts from the Infinity-Fire, meaning all spot fires around the cosmos are generated from the same eternal flame.

The Infinity-Fire is an eternal fire that flickers across the web of neural connections revealing the interconnectedness of all consciousness across all space and time. I saw the Infinity-Fire sparking in the web of galaxy clusters during my awakening experience and I will never be the same because it revealed to me the true nature of reality. Every being, every star, and every quantum particle has the Infinity-Fire interwoven into its existence. When the Infinity-Fire is broken down to its foundational essence, its structure is sacred geometry and its vibration is unconditional love. Unconditional love is what makes the universe breathe with life! Just like the torching tree throws embers that breathe life into new forest fires, the Infinity-Fire throws embers into the universe that create every human's Heart-Fire. Unconditional love is the vibration of the Infinity-Fire while compassion (love plus understanding) is what drives action. When you base all actions on unconditional love and purposeful compassion, you are living your dharma—your soul's purpose—and you are fulfilling your soul's contract.

The Infinity-Fire is only understood by the higher-self because the rational mind will resist understanding the infinite flow of unconditional love. It can be baffling to realize how much love there truly is in the universe. When I felt unconditional love from my higher-self, I developed compassion for every being because I realized what unconditional love felt like at the soul level. *Experiencing this for yourself will make you cry with joy!* I wanted to express my every thought and every action with this vibration because spreading love and compassion is the paramount lesson of the Infinity-Fire. *Compassion—love plus understanding—is the force that creates action in the universe and unconditional love is the conduit through which compassion moves.*

When I was on my cosmic journey during my awakening experience, I discovered my answers to the universe when I saw a neural network of super consciousness. I realized that the entire cosmos is alive, and everything is energy! When I got that answer during my visionary state, I instantly felt like I was going to explode from the intense feeling of unconditional love in every quantum particle and super massive black hole. With my new understanding, I also felt so much love in the universe that I had no doubt that there is more than enough love in existence for all humans to heal, to be healthy, and to be safe and joyful.

When I found unconditional love to be at the basis of all action—even within my own life—I integrated the lessons that the Infinity-Fire showed me. The integration of the Infinity-Fire allowed me to return to my higher-self and become one with my spiritual companion—the natural state of life that humans forget when we are born. This connection re-forged an alliance between my Heart-Fire, my higher-self, and the Infinity-Fire, which resulted in a higher state of consciousness. The alliance allowed my highest-self to enter my body and I began to see all of the self-work I needed to match the vibration of the Infinity-Fire. I felt a twin spark (Infinity-Fire and Heart-Fire) when my consciousness merged with the Infinity-Fire to create a spiraling energetic explosion of extraordinary potential. When the twin sparks are spiraled into a single spiritual essence (a human being), true understanding can become reality and all actions flow from unconditional love and compassion.

The merging spiraled essence is similar to the Infinity-Fire that sparks the divine consciousness in all of reality. Once the entangled twin spark is seated in the body, it will bring about remembrance, and knowing your true soul's nature is a profound experience. Remembering that our connection to the divine is all humanity needs to feel spiritually nourished—while also losing body consciousness—will change your entire outlook on life. You are not a body but rather a soul that is acting on the stage of life until your light is called back home to its source. *When your point of reference in life is from soul consciousness, you will feel unconditional love and complete fulfillment in every moment, breath, and action. This is the definition of enlightenment.* I have only had glimpses of this and even that was enough to inspire the deepest changes in my mind, body, and spirit.

The connection to Infinity-Fire helps you feel unconditional love for yourself and teaches you to act from a place of compassion. The Infinity-Fire alliance gives you access to ancient wisdom that only your heart can read, which allows you to use your Heart-Fire skills to find your soul's contract. Remember: the soul's contract is purposeful action driven by the core principles of the Infinity-Fire. Your original instruction lies in understanding your true purpose on the planet and releasing yourself to the influence of your Heart-Fire as you walk the path of devotion to unconditional love and compassion.

Your soul's contract is an agreement between your Heart-Fire and the Infinity-Fire that was forgotten when you were born. One of the challenges of your time on Earth is finding the contract of your original instructions. Your original instructions are the state of being, actions, and beliefs that allow you to flow with ease into your highest potential in all levels of life. There are four overarching levels of life: physical, mental, emotional, and spiritual. As you experience this way of living and listen to your heart, miracles will appear in your life and your life will advance on all four levels.

Let's look at each level in a little more depth. In the spiritual level, you connect with the Infinity-Fire and your higher-self. In the mental level, you have power over your thoughts and understand the ability of the mind to manifest a positive reality. The emotional level is about understanding that the vibration of your heart and emotion creates the law of attraction. In the physical level, you will see that actions speak louder than words and your actions are a reflection of your inner landscape. Physical health is about knowing that living balanced and healthily is a large part of being happy. You must understand the effects that your environment can have on your mind, body, and spirit, and then acknowledge that you are the average of your top-five closest relationships. The physical level is also about understanding that wealth is an abundance of opportunity, acquired food, water, shelter, education, and love—not money.

To take the levels of life to a deeper understanding, let's explore how they work. The Infinity-Fire flows unconditional love into your life at the spiritual level. At the mental level, when you are thinking in terms of the highest good for all, the energy perfectly flows to the next level. When the energy reaches the emotional level, if you have done deep self-work and released your emotional baggage (past resentment, memories that haunt you, past trauma), the energy freely flows into the physical body. When all levels of life are aligned in this way, you are wealthy, vibrant, healthy, safe, and happy.

Attaining satisfaction on all four levels takes discipline and practice every day through the remembrance of your true nature. The act of remembering your true nature as an alignment of mind, body, and spirit, and living with the intention of unconditional love and compassion is remembrance. We need to remember that life's spark comes from the Infinity-Fire and that all beings are part of the same eternal flameless fire. Remembrance is the act of connecting your soul's light to the source of light to gain the alignment of mind, body, and spirit. Connecting to the Infinity-Fire allows you to surrender any negative emotions or thoughts so you can release your mental/emotional baggage. The Infinity-Fire is the master of transmuting negativity into pure light that energizes the human spirit. Surrendering and receiving power from the Infinity-Fire is a wonderful practice that creates alignment on all levels.

Constructing a connection to the divine energy source is simple: slow your mind enough to open yourself up to the vastness of this moment, right now. Meditation is the key to accomplishing this because meditative practice slows the mind enough to unpack the layers of the human experience as if they were layers of an onion. Meditation can be achieved while walking, skiing, hiking, loving, being creative, or doing anything else that allows your mind to slide to the background. I will teach you in later chapters how best to connect your Heart-Fire to the Infinity-Fire.

PART TWO

The South—Ignite Heart-Fire

CHAPTER SIX

Heart-Fire Safety

As is the case with any type of fire, Heart-Fire requires precautions, too. The biggest safety precaution is understanding that the Infinity-Fire and Heart-Fire are flameless. This means that they guide life by fostering life's highest potential for all beings. If your Heart-Fire becomes unbalanced, you can become blocked and experience health concerns. If a mishandling occurs, fire energy can become stuck on the third eye center resulting in visions, unprotected astral projection, mania, and loss of reality. Without proper training, visions and unprotected astral protections are dangerous because they occur when you are not grounded, and you can become lost. Having protection means staying grounded while setting energetic boundaries for your mind, body, and spirit. It's important to understand the dangerous side-effects, so use the prudent precautions I have laid out and follow each exercise to completion.

Having a protection meditation that can be practiced daily is one of the best safety precautions for activating your Heart-Fire. Such a meditation creates a boundary for your energy while allowing you to stay grounded, and this is how you ward off unwanted energy. Negative energy can come to you from other people's negative emotions or any darkness in the universe. Because of this, knowing where your energy begins and ends is a clear way to stay protected. (There are additional reasons why protection is important, but since we're at the basic level of training, let's focus on your safety.)

Luckily, there is a simple method called grounding that will keep you away from any harmful effects. (Being grounded is defined as being in control of your body and mind while connecting to the energy of the earth.) In the Chinese art of moving meditation called Qigong, there are three primary Dan Tians, or energy centers. Your lower Dan Tian is in your lower abdomen just below the navel and this is your center of gravity. This is where your life force or Qi is gathered, mixed, and disseminated throughout the body. The next Dan Tian has less energy density at its center and is located in the heart region. The last Dan Tian is the least energetically dense and resides in the region of the third eye. It is important to keep your Dan Tians in a pyramid structure with the most energy residing at the bottom. The pyramid should slowly decrease in density as the energy rises. Grounding occurs when you focus your energy and re-center your energetic system to its natural state with the majority of energy residing in the lower Dan Tian. This pyramid structure is easy to maintain with daily grounding meditation and practice.

In Qigong, there exists a point directly in the center of the bottom of the foot called the bubbling well. The bubbling well is where the energy of the human body interacts with Earth's energy and grounds the human bioelectric system. In the larger picture of the human energetic system, the body acts like a conduit for energy from Father Sky to mix with energy from Mother Earth. The mixed energies from Heaven and Earth combine with your Heart-Fire to create the human experience. The human experience is a vibration because it is created from the heart center. The act of grounding guides the flow of energy from the divine to the top of your head, through your heart, and out through the perineum down an energetic grounding cord to the center of the Earth, all the while keeping its flow oriented in the most ideal direction.

Grounding should be the foundation of any spiritual practice because it keeps your soul inside your body. In addition, physical connection with the earth is beneficial due to the negative ions that the human body absorbs in a natural setting.[10] Finding a grounded state will build a solid foundation in the mind, body, and spirit. You want to be grounded so you can trust your Heart-Fire skills because your connection with the earth is the substructure of a positive spiritual practice. Being grounded brings a calming, peaceful state inside your nervous system and opens the body to divine energy, and this allows more positive thinking, feeling, and believing to guide you. This is why grounding is the foundation of mentally and emotionally trusting yourself.

When a Chātra is grounded, room is revealed to start focusing on the gut. In Qigong, the origin of your chi is the lower Dan Tian because your center of gravity just below the navel is where all spiritual practice originates. In Chinese medicine, the gut is the center of everything in mind, body, and spirit. Modern science has recently revealed that the gut has more neurons than the brain and "talks" to the brain through a newly discovered circuit.[11] I have realized that there is a reason I have been fighting fire with my gut my entire career: it's part of my brain! The gut is an intuitive sense organ of the human body and it will tell you when there is danger or peace and the ways in which you can take the next step toward optimal survival. When your gut "turns inside out" or when you get "butterflies", it is a sign that you need to pay attention to your environmental circumstances. The gut is talking to your brain because it can sense things in the environment around you that your normal eyes, ears, and smell cannot. The gut can tell you what will happen in the immediate future if you tune in to it. The key, however, is to turn down the chatter flowing along in your mind's river of thoughts.

As you travel up the body, the next brain center is your heart center. The heart is certainly sophisticated enough to qualify as a "heart-brain"[12] as it has almost as many neurons as the brain. The heart is the emotional center of the body and acts like a tuning fork of the human experience. When your heart is vibrating at a higher frequency, you will have joyful emotions that spread throughout your adjacent environment. A deeper question to ask is whether or not the universe around you is vibrating at this frequency and you are simply allowing your heart to tune in. Conversely, when your heart is vibrating in a lower frequency, you will experience worry, anger, or other negative emotions.

For some people, these emotions and frequencies begin as fleeting images and eventually translate into full-fledged thoughts. Images are the precursor to emotions, and feelings are the forbearers of thinking. Remember: through quantum mechanics, thoughts combined with emotions create your reality.[13] Our emotions dictate the vibration of our reality while thoughts solidify our manifestation of reality. This is the basic rule for the law of attraction. Connecting to the heart vibration and learning to change the frequency to unconditional love and compassion will aid you in manifesting your soul's mission.

Furthermore, when the seeker learns to link all three brains—the gut, heart, and brain—the result is an all-encompassing body-brain that can receive information from the environment in several different ways. To triangulate is to listen to inputs from three different directions and it paints a more accurate picture of your overall experience. Using your gut for intuition, your heart for emotional intelligence, and your brain for cognitive function creates the proper checks and balances when governing yourself. Your gut can turn inside out telling you to listen to your heart, and then your heart's feelings have to be deciphered and overlaid with physical reality and cognitive comparisons. All of these things work together to make a congruent decision.

Societal norms tend to dictate a reliance on the rational mind for life decisions, but we must work hard to avoid this in order to connect with our higher-selves. Turning off the mind's ever-flowing fountain of thoughts will allow the heart and gut to be heard. Once all three brains are connected and "allowed" to properly function, the seeker will form a conduit to the higher-self, opening up to ancient wisdoms because the very nature of language is that every word loses truth in translation. The only way to sync all three brains is through relaxation and meditation. You are indeed integrating your mind and body, and this will allow you to hear your higher-self for the first time.

When all three brains are connected, the seeker will open the gate for heart coherence. Heart coherence is when the heart is vibrating and beating in a positive emotion giving you a sense of well-being, and it is the next step toward your Heart-Fire activation. Simply breathe into your heart center and hold love for something like a pet or spouse.[14] This is the one-minute method that is recommended by the Heart Math Institute to achieve heart coherence.

A seeker of truth and harmony wants to integrate the gut, heart, and brain because it unlocks sensory inputs that are typically blocked by the rational mind. Unconsciously blocking input from your entire nervous system is a learned skill in the industrious age of production. Industrious production does not want you to truly feel your environment because this technique of living doesn't conform to the accepted picture of reality. The goal of living using your gut, heart, and brain is to achieve the feeling of Pono; feeling right with self on all levels of life. By integrating the entire nervous system, you will open the gate to Heart-Fire activation and heart coherence, and you will allow the process of opening your heart center to begin. Heart-Fire activation will also strengthen your spiritual practice by bringing unconditional love and compassion into your life. Remember: unconditional love and compassion are the vibrations and frequencies that manifest your soul's contract! By holding this vibration, you are commanding your dreams and your future. Even right now, your highest potential is right in front of you, lingering behind a veil. It is simply vibrating at a higher frequency and to obtain it, all you have to do is match that vibration. When your thoughts and emotions are equal to your highest frequency, you will activate your Heart-Fire and miracles will happen.

How do you begin to open the gates to Heart-Fire activation?

The first steps to activating your Heart-Fire Skills are as follows:

1. Practice the **Protection Meditation.**

2. Practice the **Grounding Meditation** every day.

3. Practice **relaxation through mindfulness** during daily activities.

Protection & Grounding Meditation
Protection & Grounding Meditation
Download the guided meditations at:
https://bit.ly/Grounding-Meditation-Like-a-tree
https://bit.ly/Protection-Guided-Meditation

The benefits of grounding come from negative ion exposure radiating from the earth. Experiencing grounding calms the nervous system and improves overall psychological health. This practice keeps the natural pyramid structure of the three Dan Tians in place. The standing tree practice will nourish the entire body system while recycling negative emotions through Mother Earth.

Relaxation Through Mindful Activity During the Day

To recap: Relaxation through moving mindfulness is called flow. Flow is a balanced ratio of challenge versus skill. It is achieved in an activity where you are so focused on the task that you lose sense of time. In essence, you forget what you are doing, and the body freely moves without the impediments of the active mind. This is the root of relaxation through mindfulness! If you can achieve flow-state while walking, hiking, skiing, or participating in any activity you enjoy, keep doing it! Flow as much as possible. Flowing is about connecting to the higher power through relaxed meditation in motion.

CHAPTER SEVEN

Mind-Body-Spirit Purification

In this chapter I will teach you the basics of the triangle of self-love. This triangle is the foundation that will give you the stability to go a layer deeper into the triangles of conviction and spiritual power, which I will discuss in the next part of the book. Nutrition for the human experience encompasses all the things that you allow into your reality. A Chātra wants to purify both access points—the mind and body—and raise their vibrations to match their highest potential. This higher vibrational experience will work to tune your heart to the same frequency as your higher-self. Taking in pure nourishment for your mind and body requires practicing Heart-Fire embrace; this means taking responsibility for everything you allow into your system. (In this context, the system includes anything physical, mental, emotional, or spiritual.) Remember: no one else is responsible for what you allow into your inner structure! Being honest and respectful with yourself and owning your intake is the only way to achieve your best day. Heart-Fire embrace, honesty, and persistence will pave the way for purification.

Mind-body-spirit purification will give you resounding results in thoughts, feelings, and behaviors. When these systems are purified, you will experience positive thoughts and contagious loving feelings, and your actions will be rooted in kindness. Your mind will seem light and easier to quiet while your body will feel strong and healthy, and your actions will be admirable. The preparation process for this kind of purification takes time and practice. You will know you are ready for Heart-Fire activation when your thoughts are healthy, safe, and happy, and you feel deep, unconditional love for yourself. You will know you've achieved this when you find yourself practicing random acts of kindness and demonstrating compassionate actions for the highest good for all. Even right now, you know deep within your heart that you are ready for an upgrade, so let's get started! Purifying the mind-body-spirit begins with changing the three diets.

1. The diet of the **mind** consists of your thoughts, the media you choose to consume, conversations with which you engage, the music you listen to, and the books you read. It also includes how often you practice meditation and how well you process the information you receive from the outside world. (This book is part of your mind's diet because I am accessing your mind right now!)

2. The diet of the **body** is broken down into the air you breathe, the water you drink, and the food you eat. It also includes the relationships you cultivate and the emotions you feel on a daily basis. (The way you feel about this book is altering your body's diet right now!)

3. The **spiritual** diet directly correlates to the strength of your alliance with your higher-self and the Infinity-Fire. Your devotion to unconditional love and compassion is the ultimate measurement of spiritual health, and your conviction to the divine source is the litmus test for your spiritual fitness.

As you experience the purification process, you will feel the results of health, safety, and happiness while your heart opens to the highest good for all. What I learned from my own purification process is that it is not easy, and it takes hard work. Also, with honest self-reflection, Heart-Fire embrace, and consistent drive, you will be able to achieve your highest potential. After the purification of your mind-body-spirit, you will have the same vibration as your highest-self, and you will easily manifest your highest potential for the highest good for all. You will experience the emergence of your spiritual connection!

So, let's discuss the best ways to purify your mind, body, and spirit:

How to Purify Your Mind

- Use affirmations every day such as, "I am healthy, safe and happy" to override any negative thinking

  o Before you allow negative thoughts to enter and flourish in your mind, change the moment with a positive affirmation

- Reduce or eliminate the intake of any media, conversations, or relationships that carry negative energy

  o This will allow room for positive vibrations in your life

- Practice meditation every day to soothe the mind

  o Embracing silence in nature will calm the mind even further

- Discern what information is valuable and worth your time in this overwhelming age of instant and constant information

- Always see the positive outcome in every situation

- Try a digital detox—it's a powerful technique to reset the habits of your informational diet

  o Start with a twenty-one-day digital detox challenge

Try a "Prescribed Fire" for Your Mind

A prescribed fire is a way to use fire as a tool on the landscape. In this instance, fire is a positive tool that cleans the forest in a helpful way. In wildland firefighting, we use prescribed fires to clear the built-up young trees that connect the ground to the top of the forest canopy. Leaving these untouched is hazardous because they provide the perfect ladder for fire to climb during extreme weather conditions. When the conditions are right, planned, and monitored, fire can be used to clean the woods. When fire is absent from any landscape for too long, the forest becomes unhealthy with overgrowth.

This principle is the same in your mind. If you don't clear out space in your mind, everything becomes cluttered and a perfect ladder is formed for negative emotions to climb into the forefront of your experience. Visualizing fire (and using fire as a tool in your mind in the same way that fire managers use real fire to clean the landscape) is a powerful technique to clear out the heaviness of your thoughts.

A guided meditation is what you need to efficiently use fire under the right conditions while keeping it contained in order to prioritize safety. Real fire in the mountains is different than a fire in your mind because the fire in your mind is safe and supports life.

Prescribed Fire for Your Mind: Download the guided meditation at:

https://bit.ly/Prescribed-Fire-Guided-Meditation

How to Purify Your Body

- Focus on your nourishment in this order: Breath, Water, Food, Sleep, Exercise, and Love

  o This order is critical because it is arranged in importance according to survival

- Practice deep abdominal breathing during your daily meditation practice[15]

- Drink clean water that you have blessed as it has powerful effects beyond hydration[16]

  o Tape a message of LOVE or GRATITUDE on your water bottle or pray over your water

- I hold my glass of water in my left hand and practice the following prayer every day: "I honor the space in which you exist; please nourish my mind, body, and spirit. I love you; thank you. Please protect me and my loved ones. You have sacred geometry. I honor the space in which you exist." —Add more specific prayers when needed.

- Filtering contaminants from our water is most important in our polluted world[17]

- Eating a balanced diet for *your* body is critical. Don't blindly follow a fad diet like paleo, vegan, etc.[18]

  o Practice the HEART Diet:

    - Eat foods that are: **H**ydrating, **H**olistic, and **H**ealthy

    - **E**nergetic and **E**njoyable

    - **A**bundant in nutrition

    - Take time to: **R**ead your body and listen to it

    - **T**hank your food and pray

o Try making a food journal to record how you feel twenty minutes after every meal. Writing in your journal about the ways in which food makes you feel will help you identify foods that are healthy for *you*. (Record any negative side-effects and make a note to avoid that food. Conversely, if there is a food that makes you feel amazing and you find yourself craving it, then make a note and eat more of that food. Your body will sometimes crave foods that it needs but this is not the same thing as sugar cravings.)

As beautiful and magnificent as the human body is, humans are more than a body. Humanity is so special because we are a perfect mixture of mind, body, and spirit. When the mind, body, and spirit are aligned with the divine, we are capable of expanding our Heart-Fire to the entire body which allows us to see the true nature of the human condition. This "true-nature-remembrance" is, in essence, the *awakening*. This means that you understand that you are not simply a body, but rather, you are a spiritual being *learning through* a body for a period of time on this Earth. When this lesson is fully integrated and accepted, the mind-body-spirit is purified, and the highest-self is accessible. When we *know* that our body is temporary and our consciousness is eternal, we can see the body as a vessel for divine energy during meditation and truly receive golden light from the Infinity-Fire. This "spiritual vitamin D" is the greatest source of nourishment in the universe because it is the most potent version of unconditional love and compassion, and it raises the soul's vibration so high that anything that doesn't serve you falls away and you are restored to your original instructions. *The golden light is what heals your mind, body, and spirit.*

I refer to this golden light as "the golden fire"; a flameless fire, and it's sourced from the Infinity-Fire. But, remember—this is a flameless fire so harm won't befall you and you will only receive healing and love. You will know the Infinity-Fire has encapsulated your energetic body when you feel a euphoric wave roll down your spine. This wave is often accompanied by tears of joy, a smile, laughter, or a feeling of oneness. In reality, your Heart-Fire is but a shard of the Infinity-Fire. We are a fractal (a geometric pattern that repeats on all levels for infinity) of the Infinity-Fire; we are one.

Receiving the golden fire raises your vibrational field so high that heavy thoughts, feelings, and behaviors fall away. This type of energy is for the highest good for all, so it naturally releases darkness to be recycled by the Infinity-Fire. This level of connection to the Infinity-Fire occurs when you are shown that you are not a body but rather a consciousness *inside* a body that is created to learn lessons that cannot be learned in the higher dimensions. You will experience that you are an infinite consciousness swirling with unconditional love and sacred geometry. By owning your nature as a spiritual being, it is easy to release lower vibrations because, with unconditional love permeating throughout your being, you will understand that even the most negative vibrations have love at their deepest core. Understanding that even negativity has love at its core is the point when you can just let go. This letting go is when the lower vibrations are surrendered to a higher power. Connecting and awakening to your true spiritual nature is the doorway to your Heart-Fire skills.

Golden Fire without a Flame: Download the guided meditation at: https://bit.ly/Golden-Fire-Guided-Meditation

CHAPTER EIGHT

Detoxify Your Heart

My experience with heart detoxification took time and practice, but the fastest way you can achieve it is through a technique called Mental Emotional Release (MER), also known as Timeline Therapy. The basic idea of the technique is that you travel back through your timeline to a root event that is causing emotional pain. You see the event from a distant view, harness the lessons you needed to learn, and release the emotions behind the event. Letting go of the emotions behind a traumatic event almost instantly changes your vibration.

The universe is based on vibrations, and to change my vibration I had to delve deep into release-work to break down the upper-limiting subconscious walls that I built for myself. I discovered that I didn't have just one wall that was separating me from my highest potential, but rather, I had many that worked together to form a maze that required me to confront my inner child and work with my anger. My anger constantly erected roadblocks and lowered my vibration to the point that I couldn't hear my Heart-Fire. Detoxifying my heart required acupuncture, meditation, Ho'oponopono, hypnosis, MER, and honesty, fully supported by the Heart-Fire embrace of my life. Every day proved to be an act of courageous folly. I stumbled my way through my heart detoxification so that you could read this book and detox with grace. *The most valuable lesson I can share from the detoxification of my heart is that the fabric of the universe is comprised of unconditional love and all the actions that move through this medium are compassionate exertion.* Unconditional love and compassion are vibrations, and the detoxification of your heart is ultimately achieved when your heart is returned to this specific vibration.

Preparing for detoxification requires purifying the mind, body, and spirit, as discussed in the previous chapter. Detoxifying your heart is the way in which you clear all of the emotional blockages that hold you back from your highest potential. The heart is a tuning fork and detoxifying it requires clearing away the sludge that enrobes it while allowing the universal vibration of unconditional love and compassion to ring inside you. Surrendering your emotional sludge to the Infinity-Fire is the basic tool for detoxifying your heart. Fully ceasing your resistance to the Infinity-Fire while co-creating a new self-image takes courage because you have to face yourself. Surrendering your lower vibrational feelings to the Infinity-Fire will return the heart to its original frequency and its original instructions. As just mentioned, the heart is a tuning fork and it resonates with vibrations—it's all a vibration. Lower vibrations are emotions that bring you down like anger, sadness, fear, guilt, shame, and hurt. Higher vibrational emotions are unconditional love and compassion, and when you hold these feelings, your heart is strong and ready for activation. When your heart is clear and open, your heart center will brightly burn, and you will feel released from lower vibrational forces. Think of your heart as a glass filled with murky water. If you want your glass to contain clear water, you need to pour out the murky water and obtain clean water from the faucet. Your faucet is the Infinity-Fire!

Once your heart is detoxified, only your limiting beliefs will hold you back from being able to hear your Heart-Fire for the first time. A limiting belief is when you make a decision to believe something that isn't true during a traumatic event in the past. In most cases, the limiting belief is so literal that you don't even realize you are carrying a lie inside your heart.

My major limiting belief was that if I was late, I was going to die. I decided to believe this lie during a fire assignment in southern Idaho. It was a hot and windy summer day in August and the sagebrush and juniper trees were explosive. I was riding along with my Engine Boss (the captain of the firetruck crew), and a taskforce leader (a field supervisor that is in charge of five to seven fire crews). We were driving up a canyon to the north of the main fire, scouting for buildings and making plans to protect structures in the canyon. Suddenly, the radio cued and Air Attack (the aerial supervisor that watches the fire and conducts air traffic control from the air) came over the radio with a voice of concern and leadership. He called out our engine number and said, "The engine in the canyon needs to get out of there now because the fire has significantly picked up and is nearing the ridge above you." The taskforce leader responded, and we started our way out of the canyon. On our way down I heard a gunshot and we slowly rolled to a stop on a two-track road in the middle of a canyon. The Engine Boss screamed, "F***! Well, we got a flat."

We jumped out of the truck to assess the situation, and sure enough we had a flat tire. We were now stranded with a brush fire at the head of the canyon, and the situation was very serious. Air Attack focused his army of helicopters on the head of the canyon to keep it from sloping over the ridge and heading straight for us. I remember the flurry of radio traffic as all flanks of the fire were being lost and operational plans started to roll back to the drawing board. It was now the afternoon and the wind picked up around this desert fire. As soon as we got the damaged tire off the truck, the fire crested the ridge and was only a quarter mile away—*much* too close given the volatility of the landscape's fuel type.

I remember the taskforce leader screaming and yelling that he was going to be late to his meeting. "I am going to be late to my briefing! F***!", he shouted. *I want to freeze the story right here. This was the exact second I made the* *decision to believe, "If I am late, I am going to die." For years going forward, I would almost get a panic attack if I was late, because deep down I thought if I was late, I was going to die. This demonstrates the literal nature of the subconscious mind, and how we create these limiting beliefs. Most limiting beliefs are from childhood and stem from occurrences before seven years old. Back to the story!* We got the tire changed in time, but we had a swarm of helicopters dropping water on the fire that was heading our way by the time we drove out of the close call.

Limiting beliefs can be hard to recognize in yourself and you won't know that you are carrying them until they are pointed out to you by a mental health professional. There are many different ways to let go of limiting beliefs through NLP and MER. Once the heart is detoxified and limiting beliefs are released, you will be able to hear your Heart-Fire for the first time and you can decide what you want to believe. When you choose to believe higher vibrational thoughts like unconditional love and compassion, you will be able to access your Heart-Fire skills. Heart-Fire skills are only possible in a higher vibrational state, including the attainment of emotions such as contentment and happiness. Finding a state that promotes higher emotional states starts with gratitude and loving yourself, moving that love to everything in the universe, and using it to compassionately act throughout your days.

Unconditional love and compassion for yourself are the root of detoxifying your heart. Heart emotions are life-affirming and when you are reconnecting to the heart for the first time, you may be faced with a wall of grief. This wall of grief will become apparent because you may realize, "Why haven't I thought, felt, and acted like this my entire life?" A reconciliation must occur to accept the time lost to lower vibrational states. It is essential to feel these emotions and work through them because there are lessons to be learned from every negative emotion. In this way of thinking, the wall of grief can be the ultimate mentor.

I caution you here: if you don't move through these negative emotions and instead choose to take spiritual shortcuts or bury difficult feelings with an addictive habit, the negativity will invariably return with a vengeance. Until you listen to your Heart-Fire, patterns will repeat, and every repetition will exponentially worsen. This is why it is common for people to connect with their Heart-Fire when they are told they have a terminal illness. In some cases, illnesses have gone into complete remission because heart paths were followed. Heart-Fire can create miracles or extraordinary synchronicities! The best practice is to feel all emotions that arise because the only way to clear an emotion is to feel it and understand its origin. However, there is a difference between feeling an emotion then releasing it and letting that feeling consume you. Once you understand its origins and have grasped the lesson behind the emotion, it is time to surrender it to the Infinity-Fire for recycling. Truly feeling emotions and being honest about them takes courage—this is a Hero's Journey all on its own.

There is a difference between feeling an emotion, finding the lesson, and releasing the thoughts, feelings, and behaviors, and holding onto an emotion for years and allowing it to eat you from the inside out. Emotions that we hold onto for a long time turn into heavy baggage and are harder to put down. Emotions are a gift, but baggage is a burden and releasing them requires different techniques. Emotions are fleeting and fluid and are more easily released by meditation, journaling, going outside, and being with loved ones. Emotions that have become baggage are stuck at the deepest subconscious levels, making it difficult to identify and isolate the issues on our own. This is why it is so hard to let go without a proper practitioner to help you.

It takes courage to reflect on the self in the present *and* in the past. Courageous self-reflection is when you identify the things that have wounded your heart and also acknowledge the hearts that you may have wounded. Making peace with these emotional low points in your life takes determination. There is no easy way to courageously reflect on negative emotions—it is simply hard work. The subconscious mind often builds a wall around these suppressed emotions and blocks you from your highest potential, but this is where healing through forgiveness is possible! The most efficient way to navigate this is through an ancient Hawaiian practice called Ho'oponopono. The basics are this: You bring everyone from the past, you send them healing light from the divine, and ask them to forgive you as you forgive them. After you give and receive forgiveness, you cut all "aka connections" (cords of light connecting to your heart centers) between you and them. This sounds simple, but the results are priceless. I technically cannot teach you this technique because I am not a Kupuna (Native Hawaiian elder), but Dr. Matt and Huna.com have the resources you need to find and apply this information.

So, why would you bother courageously reflecting and walking through a wall of forgiveness? Because, breaking down this wall is like opening your perspective to a whole new world, revealing new angles and points of view to expand your consciousness. With a clean emotional state, you will have access to your inner vision, intuition, and most of all, your Heart-Fire skills. When your baggage is gone, you will flow with ease and be content in every moment.

It is paramount that you understand the lesson to be learned from the Infinity-Fire. Remember: honesty is a necessity and self-honesty takes courage. It can be daunting and downright terrifying to be honest about how your emotional wall is reinforced around certain past events. With courage and Heart-Fire embrace, you will own those past events and be able to control your past. Every time you practice Heart-Fire embrace you build up your personal power and audacity. When you are ready, your personal power will be the ultimate driving force that allows you to simply walk through the wall of suppressed emotions. When you own your past, present, and future, then it is your time to ratify the emotional blocks that have starved you from your highest potential. After detoxifying your heart, you will be ready to break through your emotional wall and reach your highest potential!

A powerful practice to try is the act of writing and mailing letters to the people with whom you have unfinished business. In doing so, you will release resentment and your wall of emotions will start to break down. A helpful aid in this process is the use of guided meditations and Heart-Fire coaching to help you break down the reinforced walls and spur rapid and unimaginable growth. These tactics can be implemented in conjunction with the help of a professional Mental Emotional Release (MER) practitioner in a breakthrough session. A breakthrough session takes you into a deep state similar to hypnosis and allows the practitioner to guide you through a timeline empowerment process which helps you release all of the emotions tied to certain heavy events in your past. In doing so, you release anger, sadness, fear, hurt, guilt, and shame from your entire timeline and relinquish all of the limiting beliefs you have ever carried. To reinforce the transformation, the session is completed with a hypnosis to install new positive beliefs that you can carry forward. This technique can be more effective and much faster than therapy, only taking eight to sixteen hours. Similarly, working with a talented acupuncturist can be a lifesaving event when your emotions feel as if they're bringing about your demise.

Ho'oponopono with Dr Matt—Credit to Empowerment Partnership @ Huna.com:
Listen to the guided meditation at:
https://bit.ly/Hooponopono-YouTube

CHAPTER NINE

Heart-Fire Guidance for Fear Versus Love

Heart-Fire guidance is a subtle force that allows you to be decisive in the moment by using body sensations. The following strategy will show you where you have clarity, excitement, and ease, and heavy, slow, tense, or gut-wrenching upset. Your Heart-Fire guidance will expose the universal truth that all vibrations exist on a bilaterally sliding scale between love and fear. In life, all fear melts away when unconditional love is present, and conversely, love loses its power the farther you slide into fear. It's all about vibrations and the higher your vibration, the easier your path will be. Although, just as the yin and yang are interrelated, fear and love help define each other—one without the other would make for a dull experience. *The ultimate key in Heart-Fire guidance is to find unconditional love even if you're residing in the lower vibrations of fear.*

Don't worry: your Heart-Fire guidance will tell you when you're picking the easiest path or the path of flow and ease. In this way, it will also tell you when you are going head-first into resistance or achieving helpful flow states.

Flow state means being in the exact place you need to be to grow your mind, body, and spirit while doing what your Heart-Fire guides you to do. Most people experience flow states during moving meditations like Tai Chi, or when a physical challenge has a balance between challenge versus skill. Tuning into Heart-Fire guidance might give you pause as it will feel like you have an element of reservation about the guidance because you know it will be a serious challenge that will ultimately lead to greatness. There is a fine line between the trepidation of Heart-Fire guidance and unnecessary resistance that sees you banging your head against the proverbial wall. Between suffering and bliss, you will find the path of Heart-Fire guidance, and it's the place where you will feel brave for overcoming resistance and suffering, but not overwhelmed by an overzealous desire to accomplish it all.

This middle-ground of rapid growth is often felt in the gut. Following your Heart-Fire guidance forges a clear route toward heart activation because your heart and gut are your secondary brain. For sustained growth in any direction, Heart-Fire guidance requires resiliency and the right amount of challenge. A worthwhile direction takes time and effort, and you will know you are on the right path when you feel excitement and ease bubbling on a foundation of clarity.

Learning to be comfortable with the uncomfortable is the premise of your Heart-Fire guidance. Growth is never comfortable because newness is strange and unknown, and the unknown is always the hardest place to see without fear. The feeling of being uncomfortable means you are on the edge of a breakthrough; on the fringe of some unknown greatness. Remember: the darkest part of the night is just before the dawn.[19] Appropriately, the darkest part of your personal growth is just before the dawning of your breakthrough to owning your Heart-Fire—the elixir of your *Hero's Journey*. *Owning your every mistake is fairly easy, but the hardest part of ownership is owning your greatest possibilities.* Allowing yourself to deserve greatness and unconditional love is hard to accept if you are clouded by limiting beliefs! Limiting beliefs are lies that built up in your subconscious mind that you believe without a shadow of a doubt, and you believe them so that you may not even be aware of their existence. This is why it is important to have a mentor or someone that can hold up a mirror so you can see your thoughts, feelings, and beliefs in a new way.

Integrating the Infinity-Fire is an uncomfortable process because everything you thought you knew comes under question; every element of your reality is up for grabs and you find yourself walking down a trail that you have never seen before. Your previously held notions of reality are turned upside-down and new realities are revealing themselves to you. Your limiting beliefs are dismantled, and you can now create your own belief systems that benefit you. This can be uncomfortable, but it is where you will find your Heart-Fire guidance and embody your highest-self if you dare to push past the unknown. Don't forget: your highest potential lies beyond the walls of discomfort and your highest-self is the elixir of your *Hero's Journey*.

How will you know that you are on the right path or that you're on the brink of a breakthrough? You will feel a perfect tension in your gut that acknowledges the difficulty of upcoming challenges, but your heart will scream, "Yes!" You may even have goosebumps from excitement because you now see that there is a clear path to your highest potential. However, if your gut turns upside down and you feel heavy, tense, and unsure, then you have missed the exit to your path, and you need to revaluate how best to reach your higher-self. Checked by your gut and confirmed by your heart, your Heart-Fire guidance becomes your spiritual path. (Your heart knows what you need to do, and your gut will tell you how to do it!) This is the point on your journey where you can integrate the entire nervous system to sense the universe around you as a single, unified perception organ.

Heart-Fire guidance is your true guiding force and it will not lead you astray. Simply follow that which gives you clarity, excitement, and ease while also being for the highest good for all. In addition, listen to your body when you feel heavy, tense, slow, and unclear. No teacher, book, or guru can tell you where your perfect spiritual path lies; only your Heart-Fire guidance will know this. No one knows how *you* need to spiritually proceed except your higher-self and the Infinity-Fire. When you truly learn to love flowing with ease, you will develop conviction to your own path. Remember: conviction is the seed of determination and inspiration. These forces deliver perseverance and consistency which have the power to transform your dreams into reality. *Motivated convictions that are grounded in unconditional love and compassion are truly an unstoppable force.* This force will manifest your highest-self in this reality!

It is important to have personal conviction because celebrating fortitude leads to unconditional love. It takes practice to fall in love with hardship and acknowledge and accept that everything is impermanent. When you can easily visualize your unconditional love and compassion you will have confidence in your Heart-Fire guidance. Seeing a perfect life in the future and feeling that future right now will guide you in the proper direction—the direction the Infinity-Fire wants you to go. Seeing, hearing, feeling, smelling, and tasting the future are all important components to focus on as you manifest your highest potential. This method of visualized excellence helps to build the conviction that will allow you to master determination. Conviction to unconditional love and compassion is what will allow you to take your first step using your Heart-Fire guidance. Follow the uncomfortable feeling of being on the verge of something new and your path will be full of excitement and clear results. Being guided by the highest good for all will open the door to your spiritual adventure and total life fulfillment. It takes courage to leave your safety zone and courageous action is the element that builds confidence in your Heart-Fire guidance. Finding comfort in the uncomfortable and following your Heart-Fire guidance is the recipe for a spiritual awakening!

PART THREE

Activate Heart-Fire

CHAPTER TEN

Infinity-Fire in Action

Owning that you are your highest-self right now is the Heart-Fire embrace. When you begin to take true ownership of yourself, the first step is nourishing your body in the following order: breath, water, food, exercise, sleep, and love. When you begin to take control of your basic needs, you can start in on the next layer. The triangle of self-love is supported by nourishment (breath, water, food, exercise, sleep), deep love (self-love, love for others, and all beings), and accountability (staying on course with your action plan). Nourishment, deep love, and accountability are the foundation of all spiritual work.

When you embrace your Heart-Fire, you allow yourself to acknowledge your current disturbances. The lesson behind every struggle is that the uncomfortable obstacle is highlighting that which you need to work on inside yourself. The challenge in front of you is the actual story, but the lesson is the metaphor behind the story. Seeing between the lines in life is where we find beauty, inspiration, personal growth, and compassion for ourselves. Spiritual lessons are rarely spoken, but rather they are eluded to until you see the truth with your own eyes. Only when you have a true realization will you be fully able to understand. Behind every lesson is an action and without action there is no integration of the lesson. Integration leads to full body comprehension and the ability to confidently act upon experience with clarity and certainty in the future should similar situations arise. The triangle of conviction (confidence, clarity, and certainty) allows you to focus on an outcome.

Knowing the outcome you desire crystalizes your clarity, and with an outcome and a direction, you now have command of your journey and you will be ready to take action with certainty. With every step forward that you take along your path, you will build confidence. To have the success you desire, you must move forward with the awareness that the outcome is the result and achieving it takes flexibility. Adapting and changing tactics to meet the challenge is the way in which every hardship can be turned into a lesson. When flexibility becomes exhausting, it is important to persevere and always try your best because that is the expectation of the Infinity-Fire.

As we move deeper, the next layer is to build upon the foundation of the triangle of conviction with the triangle of spiritual power. This triangle is built within yourself, your highest-self, and the Infinity-Fire. To enter the triangle of spiritual power you must have confidence, clarity, and certainty within yourself. Your highest-self is what it looks, feels, and sounds like to be fulfilling your highest mission on Earth. Accessing the highest-self is accomplished by fully realizing that you are everything you could possibly be, right now. I call this the Heart-Fire embrace. From here you can then carry with you the knowing that you have everything inside of you that you need to succeed, right now. With this realization you can begin to embody your highest-self because you have the foundation of knowing your outcome and taking action with conviction. Connecting with the Infinity-Fire allows you to hear your heart whisper priceless wisdom that keeps you spiraling upward to your highest potential. Living your highest potential fosters kindness, abundance, unconditional love, personal power, health, and true fulfillment.

In Part Three: Activate Your Heart-Fire I teach you how to build the triangles of conviction and spiritual power so you can turn every struggle into a lesson and lead yourself into a purpose-filled life.

CHAPTER ELEVEN

Heart-Fire Method

To ensure you safely activate your Heart-Fire, you must follow each of these instructions in sequence and to completion. I have taken what I did to activate my Heart-Fire on the fireline and I have broken it down into a step-by-step process that will teach you how to access your own Heart-Fire. In this chapter I provide general descriptions of the techniques and a step-by-step guide followed by a recorded guided meditation link to support your learning. You can find all of the guided meditations here: https://bit.ly/Heart-Fire-Meditations-Folder

Breath Work

I can remember my first physical training (PT) hike during my first season as a wildland firefighter. I was a rookie which essentially meant that I had no idea how to manage the basics of being in the wildland fire environment. I didn't know what gear to pack, how to arrange my gear in the truck, how to properly eat, or how to successfully sleep for five hours and immediately go back to work, but most of all, I didn't know how to breathe.

On our first PT hike of that year, we hiked a mountain directly behind our station. It was towering and steep, the footing was loose, and the pitches were unnervingly severe. All of these conditions made it a perfect training ground. I put on my fresh fire pack for the first time, and I was overloaded with gear that only a rookie carries. I was nervous because I had to perform as a team member right now and for the rest of the summer; this is was my test.

From the station, we hiked through the woods across a flat for some time, and then we began the climb. Within the first ten steps on the first incline, my heartrate increased, and I started to sweat. Doubts rushed in but I kept starring at the boots of the guy in front of me to retain focus. Within a few minutes, I couldn't breathe, my legs slowed, and my muscles tightened. I was weak because I didn't yet know how to train during the winter to prepare for the summer season. As I trudged along, my boots felt like weights, my footing slipped with every step as if I was walking along a sandy beach, and I fell behind. Then it hit me—I couldn't breathe. I was tense and dizzy, and my muscles were failing from the lack of oxygen. So, I focused on my breath and the dizziness subsided. I was winded but breathing deeper and my muscle aches subsided. I got a second wind and started hiking faster, and I closed the gap with our line of firefighters. By simply focusing on my breathing technique, I changed my entire outlook on the hike. I gained confidence and it was clear to me that I was going to make it as a firefighter. I had certainty that soon I would be on top of the mountain, breathing hard and filled with the satisfaction of completing my first hike with my dream team—my fire family and crew.

Connecting with your breath is the first step in mind-body-spirit work. Your breath is life and is the conduit for energy to enter the body. Moving forward, breath work should be the foundation of every technique you undertake. Its objective is to bring more oxygen into the body which then changes the chemistry and physiology into a state that is able to receive direct knowledge from the Infinity-Fire through your Heart-Fire. As outlined below, I use two different breathing techniques for different purposes. Wim Hof breathing allows you to go deep into your body extremely fast and quickly calms your nervous system. Hawaiian Ha breathing from Dr. Matt James helps me relax deeper and breathes life into my visualizations. I present breathing options because sometimes we need to quickly change our state of being and sometimes we need to go deep into a visualization. In the end, both techniques give you the same results through different avenues.

I want you to try this technique for the first time sitting or lying down as it is possible to become lightheaded and faint the first time you try breath work. Once you are in a comfortable and safe position, focus on breathing into your belly and lower back as deeply as possible until they expand. Keep breathing in until your chest begins to expand. Keep breathing in more, all the way until your shoulders rise toward your ears.

Breathing Techniques

Wim Hof Breathing

please visit https://www.wimhofmethod.com/
*for more information**

1. Breathe into your belly, chest, and then shoulders.

2. Let it all go and relax even deeper with every breath. Don't let your breath out all of the way here. The objective is to over oxygenate your body.

3. Repeat thirty times or until you begin to feel tingles in your hands, lips, and feet.

4. On your last exhale, breathe all the way out and hold your breath as long as is comfortable (maybe ten seconds at first and then building to longer times later).

5. Breathe as deep as is possible and hold your breath as long as is comfortable. Return to normal breathing.

6. When you are holding your breath, focus on going deep inside of yourself without thoughts.

7. Repeat for three rounds.

Ha Breathing

Follow this link https://bit.ly/Ha-Breathing for ha breathing with Dr. Matt James

Credit to Empowerment Partnership @ NLP.com

1. Breathe into your belly, chest, and then shoulders.

2. Let it all go and relax even deeper with every breath.

3. When you let go of your breath, make a "haaaa" sound and breathe all the way out.

4. Repeat this thirty times.

Protect and Ground

Before I cut any tree on the wildland fireline, I looked down at the base of the tree in question. I then looked up at the top and searched for loose branches, bark, or broken limbs. Next, I walked far away and held a string with bar nuts on it (called a plum bob) to assess the lean of the tree. I then walked out to double check where the tree would fall if I correctly felled it with its lean and I searched for any aerial hazards with the potential to kick back at me. After this thorough analysis, I checked my chainsaw to see if it was sharp.

The final step was always planning an escape route and safety zone before I put any big cuts into the tree. I created a boundary just for the sawyer (the person cutting the tree) to safely work alone. This minimized the risk to others and gave me certainty that no one was in the way so I could focus on my cuts. I tied my boot laces, drank some water, ate a snack, and if it was a really high-risk tree, I even took off my fire pack. Once I carried out my routine for safety, I prepared for my cutting procedures. I drew on the tree with my chainsaw, only cutting a half-inch deep to mark my cuts before shutting off the chainsaw. Too focus my breath, I then stood at the base of the tree and took multiple deep breaths. I visualized my cuts, I heard the cracking and popping sound of the splitting wood and felt the sound of my boots as they struck the ground when I ran down my escape route. I deeply focused on the smell of cut wood mixed with saw gas to the point that I saw the vibrations at the top of the tree that occurred as I made my back cut. I first visualized the way in which the tree would fall before I executed the first cut. After I took real action to cut the tree and it landed on the ground and everything stopped moving, it was time to assess the situation, determine what went well and pinpoint what I could improve upon for my next cut as a master sawyer. At this point, I called the entire crew over and taught them what I learned from my mistakes and wins during the "stump analysis". I integrated those lessons as I moved on to the next tree, and I kept building my skills because the fact of the matter is, *no one* is a master at tree falling. The moment you think you've mastered the basics is the moment you will get killed.

The most important technique for your safety is protection and grounding. Protection is being surrounded by loving light that only lets in the good. Grounding is connecting via energetic cord to the essence of the Earth. This keeps your soul inside your body and being in your body is the foundation of physical, mental, emotional, and spiritual health. The techniques show you how to come home to yourself and define boundaries between your energy and other energies. Knowing where your energy ends and someone else's begins is *protection*. (This is not to be confused with Earthing which has similar effects.)

Protection is accomplished through visualization and meditation techniques. For example:

1. Standing tree position: feet hip width apart, knees slightly bent, spine straight, arms in front of you in a low position, elbows slightly bent, palms

open facing each other holding an imaginary ball of energy.

2. Breath work.

3. Focus on the perineum (the area between your genitals and anus) as this is an area of dense energy and the place in which you connect with the Earth's essence energy.

4. Allow a cord of light to drop down from the perineum. This cord travels through the floor, the ground, and the crust of the Earth, all the way to the center of the Earth.

5. The cord may not be perfectly centered with the core of the Earth. Center it now.

6. Visualize your name written on this cord.

7. Allow energy to flow up from the center of the Earth through the cord and into your lower abdomen.

8. This Earth energy flows up your body through every chakra, turning on each energy center.

9. When you get to the crown of the head, the Earth energy keeps flowing up past your head and activates the seven chakras above you.

10. After reaching the seventh chakra above your body, allow yourself to connect with the Infinity-Fire and bring in divine light from the heavenly energy.

11. This energy travels down all seven chakras back into your crown and down to your abdomen.

12. The Mother Earth and Father Sky energies mix in your abdomen to create a bright white light of loving compassion.

13. Allow this light to travel down to your feet and begin filling your legs with white light.

14. Allow it to fill your core, chest, arms, neck, and head.

15. The white light spills out the top of your head, covering your skin.

16. Visualize your light body coming into a fetal position and a white egg of loving light surrounding your light body.

17. You are now fully protected. Say out loud or in your in mind, "All the good gets in, only the good gets in."

Heart-Fire Embrace

Every fire assignment is training if you let it be, because every fire experience turns into a slide (a fire memory that applies to the next similar experience). For slides to be helpful to me, I had to take ownership of every experience; I had to be honest about my failures and successes to find the lesson. Every slide has a potential lesson with the ability to carry you farther along in your career. In my own career, every position I ever held required training and task books (trainee guidebooks with tasks that must be marked off by your trainer), and every position in which I moved from "trainee" to "qualified" made me take ownership. For example, I went from a squad boss (supervisor of five to seven firefighters) to the crew boss (supervisor of twenty or more firefighters on the fireline). The role of crew boss is serious because you supervise twenty firefighters on the line while also scouting ahead and gathering intel for the chain of command above you. You provide the operational leadership with feedback and identify your needs to support your twenty firefighters while also helping to plan major operations. You don't get to be a crew boss without owning your slides, because you won't improve your leadership skills without learning. Don't ever forget that learning takes failure and failure is never bad—it's only feedback! The ways in which you take that feedback and evolve will either make you a leader or a follower. If you embrace feedback, you can move into deeper layers of leadership. During my fire career, I always saw leadership as something that started within myself, and then I applied it to others around me.

The Heart-Fire embrace is the way in which you take ownership of your highest-self while embracing the fact that you are perfect exactly the way you are. By framing things in this manner, you will come to realize that you have everything you need to be successful. There is always self-work to be done to manifest your highest-self but embracing that you are your highest-self right *now* is the Heart-Fire embrace. Follow along with the steps below to reach your Heart-Fire embrace:

1. Breath work.

2. Protect and ground.

3. Heart Math: focus on your heart center and visualize someone you love more than anything until you feel a heat in your chest.

4. Forgive yourself with a Hawaiian prayer, "I am sorry, please forgive me, I love you, thank you." You may have to repeat this mantra and visualize yourself being forgiven by your highest-self. (Practicing Ho'oponopono with Dr. Matt's audio or YouTube video will make this step faster and easier.)

5. Allow yourself to feel unconditional love being poured on top of your head and filling your entire body until you are bursting with divine light.

6. Send this light from the divine source to the ones you love in the form of a beam of compassion.

Connecting with the Infinity-Fire

My favorite task as a wildland firefighter was always being Fire Effects Monitor. The duties included hiking deep into wilderness to watch, measure, predict, and map wildland fires. It is not about fighting the fire, but rather it is about studying it. Without the chainsaw, helicopters, and radios blaring in my ears, I was able to see deeper into the lessons the fire was teaching me. I could focus on the fire as a natural event and not as a conflict between humans and nature. As a Fire Effects Monitor, I watched mountain fires sweep across entire timber stands while I filmed and took notes. I was able to see every little detail because I had time to listen and discern the deeper meaning behind the lesson that nature was teaching me. I recorded the weather on the hour, drew pictures of the smoke columns, and wrote up technical reports to describe the ecological effects on the landscape.

The Infinity-Fire is the divine source of your Heart-Fire and connecting with the Infinity-Fire opens your Heart-Fire to the communication of wisdom. By building this connection, you are acquiring heart knowledge and ancient wisdom that will serve you on your path to fulfilling your purpose. Ultimately, this technique is the way in which you receive your original instructions. Try it with the following steps:

1. Breath work.

2. Protect and ground.

3. Heart-Fire Embrace.

4. Infinity-Fire Insight: this is when you become aware of the Infinity-Fire in a way that makes you believe in a higher power. This awareness allows you to have a deeper connection to the Infinity-Fire that you will feel inside your body. It will feel like a warm tingling of love that heals all wounds within the mind, body, and spirit. To gain the Infinity-Fire Insight, you will say out loud, "I want to connect with the Infinity-Fire and receive my Heart Knowledge."

5. Repeat this saying until you feel a wave of euphoria roll down your spine. A smile will be irresistible, and you will feel so much love for yourself and others that you will believe it with your entire heart.

6. If the feeling in your body hasn't arrived yet, keep letting go. Go back to the Heart-Fire Embrace

and forgive yourself, let go, and detoxify your heart.

Finding Heart Clarity

As a firing boss, I had to understand fire on the landscape enough to direct other firefighters how best to apply fire in the field. When lighting off thousands of acres for ecological benefits or hazard fuel reduction, I had to know how hot to burn the forest. I had to know how far apart my strips of fire (firefighters lighting fires in a row across a mountain) had to be. The wider the strips, the more momentum the fire builds and the hotter it gets. I had to know which way the wind was blowing at any given second and change tactics accordingly.

There is no way to see all the factors required of a burning operation without having clarity on the boundaries, weather, firing pattern (width and direction of strips), crew morale, time of year, and years of experience watching fire. I needed a picture of what the project was to look like at the end, I had to know how the firing team was going to execute the operation, and I had to explain to every subordinate why we were creating more elk habitat.

Finding Heart Clarity is possible when you have a strong connection to the Infinity-Fire and you are open to communication from the Infinity-Fire. Heart Clarity will help you see what fulfillment looks like through the purpose and end-state of your Heart Calling. A Heart Calling is a mission for the highest good for all that gives you clarity and purpose while fulfilling you on all levels of life. Try it with the following steps:

1. Breath work.

2. Protect and Ground.

3. Heart-Fire Embrace.

4. Connecting with the Infinity-Fire.

5. Heart Listening: ask a question to the Infinity-Fire after connecting and then listen with your entire nervous system. Focus on what you think, feel, hear, or see by using your brain, heart, or gut. Heart Listening is the way in which you become deeply in touch with your own Heart Calling, and this will give you clarity. The clarity of your purpose gives you personal power, confidence, and an aim with intention. Ask out loud and listen with your entire being, and you will hear an answer.

Heart Learning

At the end of every fire shift, the entire fire team comes together to talk about the day. This is called an after-action review, or an AAR. We asked questions, we talked about what we learned, and we figured out what we could do better. Firefighters embrace their mistakes so they can learn faster and become better versions of themselves with every fire they face. However, the only way that the AAR is honorable and strengthens the team is when the *entire* team listens to each other's struggles. *The engine crew faced a failing water pump in the middle of a critical operation. The sawyer teams dodged a felled tree as it came down backwards over a road. The helicopter crew had to quickly adapt when their water bucket broke in the river.* The most critical part of the AAR was listening to the deeper particulars of how the firefighters were feeling during their problems, stress, fear, and doubt, and the ways in which they overcame it. Uniting as a team always demonstrated how any obstacle could be turned into an opportunity.

Heart Learning is when you look past your physical experience to see the deeper lessons in life. These lessons can bring peace to suffering within your physical, mental, emotional, or spiritual experiences. Heart Learning is critical to personal growth and the lessons are the steppingstones to the next layer of this practice. Don't forget that there is always a layer deeper and a lesson beyond the next lesson! When you begin to remember that we are on Earth to learn lessons and grow, your Heart Learning will increase because you will look for the lesson in everything. Try the following steps to unlock your Heart Learning:

1. Breath work.

2. Protect and Ground.

3. Heart-Fire Embrace.

4. Focus on an event or a hard time in life that brought you suffering. To build confidence, begin with something less intense before you go deeper into events that have broken your heart. It is important to see this event from far away. Allow this event to be in front of you and below you. Major emotions and events will require Mental Emotional Release and Ho'oponopono to heal.

5. Ask a question about the deeper meaning of this lesson and use your Heart Listening skills.

6. When you acquire Heart Knowledge from your Heart Listening, you will need to take action to integrate the lesson learned.

7. This action will lead to a series of actions which will give you a direction to start walking toward. This is your Heart's Calling.

Sensing Danger

Sensing danger is a practical skill that I acquired and field-tested on wildland fire assignments. Danger is defined as the possibility of harm to your mind, body, or spirit and can include physical, emotional, or spiritual threats. When I sense danger, the first thing I do is protect and ground. When you have practiced seeing with your Heart-Fire, you will be able to see danger with your mind's eye. The best way to sense danger is through a combination of *seeing* and assessing tension felt in the gut. As a wildland firefighter, I always tested trees that I was ordered to cut down. I stood next to the tree, took a deep breath, allowed my roots to grow, and focused on my lower abdomen. I asked my gut, "Am I safe?" and I felt the response in my stomach area. Light tension meant that I was in danger, but the possibility of death was low to moderate. Conversely, if I felt like my stomach turned inside out or I wanted to throw up, I knew I had to say, "No" to that tree because it was dangerous and the possibility of death was high.

I once made a split-second decision as the Incident Commander (IC) on a fire that saved the lives of everyone on my crew. It was a hot summer in August somewhere in the rugged mountains of Montana and there was a report of smoke. I was the IC on a helicopter crew that day and we were dispatched to the call. As the IC, I flew in the back seat on the left side of the helicopter and our flight in took about thirty minutes. By the time we started circling the new fire, it was small and looked like nothing we couldn't handle. Ground forces were hiking and we were called off because they had the fire handled—or so they thought. Before we could land back at the helibase, the ground forces called us back to the fire saying that they needed air support via bucket drops. So, we turned around and headed back to a fire that was no longer small. It had ballooned to acres in size and was torching trees as it worked its way up to a crackling sprint. The "stick"—two firefighters with two days of gear—were dropped off so we could assist the ground forces.

By the time I arrived on scene on the ground, the fire had grown to three acres. We put in some line for a few hours and then it got too dark to work so we bedded down for the night. The next morning, the fire had grown both in acreage and in complexity. This meant that the situation required the next level of management. I was now the IC trainee which meant I was responsible for the fire and everyone on it, but I had a trainer. (I was still training to be fully qualified as an IC at this level of complexity, but I felt confident.) The fire was active that morning, so we immediately ordered aircraft. We ordered a hotshot crew the night before that was just showing up on scene to get briefed for the day, and our air support arrived shortly after. Air attack informed us that we needed to "order the world"—call in the help of everything in the area with the capacity to drop water— so we did. We had three single-engine air tankers (similar to crop dusters except with retardant) and two heavy helicopters, and we also got the assistance of four drops from a retrofitted Boeing 737 that dumped a mile of retardant. Even still, with every air drop, the fire grew.

I was nervous now. There was only one road out of the fire, and it was one-way, very slow, and it required four-wheel drive to safely navigate. The hotshots arrived and put in some line down the flank opposite the one being tended to from above. By this time, the fire was running on all sides. Even with continued air support, the fire grew, and it became obvious to me that the lives of everyone on the fire rested on the decisions before me. I took a deep breath, I stood in front of the forest fire, and I focused on my gut. I asked the fire if I was safe and my gut began to turn with nervousness, uncertainty, confusion, and angst. I felt the urge to vomit just as the fire began to blow up even more, and there was a split-second pause in which I envisioned the fire crossing our escape route. My radio crackled with a burst of communication and right then I called everyone to disengage and retreat. My heart raced as the retreat unfolded, I was sweaty, my voice weakened with radio overuse, and my hands cramped from writing so many notes. While all of my forces safely made it out, within an hour the fire became completely uncontained and burned over the road. It most certainly would have cut off all of my firefighters from safety. Just as my gut said, we were not safe on that fire and the decision I made that day saved everyone's lives.

You can utilize this danger assessment with anything in life from a road you're supposed to drive down, to a new friend you're unsure about, to a new romantic relationship, or any life decision that feels like a crossroads. Asking the gut, "Am I safe?" is a powerful practice and can offer you protection in most situations. Try these steps to assess danger:

1. Breath Work.

2. Protect and Ground.

3. Connecting with the Infinity-Fire.

4. Use Finding Heart Clarity in the context of being safe. Simply ask, "Is this good for me? Am I safe?"

5. Use Heart Listening to see, hear, or feel your answer.

6. Sensing danger will help finetune your direction and keep you safe during your journey toward your Heart's Calling.

Finding Nourishment

Finding nourishment of the non-food variety is what your mind, body, and spirit need to recharge, and it is a very real component of life. Obtaining the necessary components for growth and well-being is my definition for finding nourishment. This type of nourishment can take the form of personal time, time in nature, a dog-walking break, journaling, yoga class, or anything else that lights up your soul. Ask yourself, *"What needs of mine are not being met?"* (Even though these needs are meant to be of the mind, body, and spirit, you can also use this assessment technique to pinpoint the foods that your body needs.) Understanding the nourishment that your mind, body, and spirit needs is simple when you ask your higher-self. All you have to do is connect with your highest possibility and ask this supreme version of yourself for the answer to a question that will serve the highest good for all.

However, connecting to the higher-self is only possible after you detoxify your heart because there has to be space in your heart for your true self to emerge. The true soul needs a higher vibrational field to manifest and when the heart-space is filled with negative emotions, the vibrations are too low for the emergence of your higher-self. Negative emotions and limiting beliefs block the higher-self from communicating with you! (We need only to look around at the state of our current world to know that this is true.)

So, practice detoxifying your heart before you practice finding nourishment. You can ask any question that fits the situation, such as: *What foods do I need to heal myself? What do I need in order to overcome my depression? Is this relationship serving me? At this junction in life, which turn do I take?* Any question that serves you in the moment will be your best guide. Your higher-self will guide you to the best possible nourishment!

During my first summer as a wildland firefighter, one of the hardest fire assignments I can remember was the fire I described earlier. We had a hard morning workout, we chain sawed all day, and just as we were getting off work, we received a fire call that required us to work for another ten hours fighting fire until late in the night. We stayed on that fire for two weeks and camped at ten thousand feet at night. Between the work, the elevation, poor nutrition, poor sleep, and constant smoke, I became exhausted beyond any exhaustion I'd experienced before. There was even a day when I was barely able to stand. The task for that day was to grid (walk in horizontal lines looking for spot fires), which is one of the most tiring things a wildland firefighter can do. I couldn't keep up in the line, I was nauseated, I felt sick, and I teetered on the verge of giving up. I tried eating more food and drinking more water, but nothing worked. I finally just laid down supine on the ground, and my crew boss said, "If you can't do the work then we need to send you to medical." I replied, "I can do it, I just need to lay here for fifteen minutes." So, I did; I let everything go, I closed my eyes, and I rested my soul for fifteen minutes. Now I know that I was meditating and grounding myself into the earth, but at the time, I had no concept of those techniques. I simply listened to my heart when it said that I had to lay on my back right away. Because I did that, I felt so much better and I was able to keep up with my work for the rest of the day! Try the following steps to find your own nourishment:

1. Breath work.

2. Protect and Ground.

3. Heart Math.

4. Connecting with the Infinity-Fire.

5. Use Heart Clarity to ask what it is that you need to nourish your mind, body, and spirit. This can be in the form of certain foods, but more importantly, it should include activities that nourish you from the inside out.

6. Heart Listening.

7. Take action.

8. Finding Nourishment will sustain your journey toward your Heart's Calling.

Heart Confidence

During the initial test for my master sawyer qualification, I thought I failed so many times. The trees I had to cut were on the edge of my comfort zone, three experts stood there evaluating me, and I was under so much pressure. My first tree fell before I finished my back cut, and my holding wood (the wood in the middle of the tree that acts as a hinge) was uneven. When I cut up the bole (stem) of the tree, I threw my chain. (This is when a chainsaw chain comes off the bar and when this happens, it shuts down all operations until it can be fixed.) My next tree was one of the most complex cuts I had ever done. The tree spanned twelve feet from the stump to the top which meant I needed a twenty-four-foot wide lane of land to fell it. That tree went perfectly, and I passed.

The following year I moved to a new forest and I had to repeat the same test all over again with different rules and new evaluators. I was still nervous the second time around and I failed the test even though my previous evaluations were more difficult. The following season I moved forests again and I repeated the experience with new rules and new evaluators—this time I passed. Every time I moved forests I had to undergo the same test. Each evaluation was a learning opportunity because every evaluator is different, and every region and forest have different rules. In wildland firefighting, every tree is a new test and major mistakes can lead to death.

Heart Confidence is when you take action, learn lessons, adapt, improvise, and succeed over and over again. Every path along every journey has obstacles, and Heart Confidence is built by turning those obstacles into opportunities. Try the following steps to find your Heart Confidence:

1. Take action.

2. Journal about what, when, why, and where you can improve.

3. Breath work.

4. Protect and Ground.

5. Heart-Fire Embrace.

6. Heart Listening.

7. Heart Learning.

8. Adapt and overcome the obstacles that held you back from taking more action toward your Heart's Calling.

9. Take more action.

Heart Certainty

Every tree I ever cut was a test and each one helped me to grow stronger as a sawyer. As my confidence grew, I began to teach others my sawyer skills because I felt certain about the safest way to cut trees. Teaching others opened up opportunities for me to learn more about cutting trees as it helped me to slow the process down and go step-by-step through motions that I myself conducted through muscle memory. By seeing my own step-by-step process on a white board, I discovered the ways in which I could improve even more. I took those lessons to the field and explored, changed, learned, and created more lessons for myself and my future chainsaw students.

Heart Certainty is when you repeatedly build Heart Confidence, have Heart Clarity, and walk every day toward your Heart's Calling. Heart Certainty is obtained by integrating all the Heart-Fire skills I have given you and in doing so, you will be able to successfully adapt any Heart-Fire skill to any situation with seamless transitions. With repetition, all these Heart-Fire skills will become automatic, faster, stronger, and more powerful. The more success you build upon, the more Heart Confidence you will gain. Heart Certainty is a journey toward mastery, and it will take time! Try the following steps to discover your own Heart Certainty:

1. Heart Confidence.

2. Repetition and confirmation of success is what builds your Heart Confidence. This is when your Heart-Fire skills will start to grow stronger and you will gain more Infinity-Fire Insight and Heart Knowledge every day.

3. Applying your Infinity-Fire Insight and Heart Knowledge every day will give you certainty of

your Heart's Calling and certainty in the direction you are traveling.

*You can find all of these meditations at https://bit.ly/Heart-Fire-Meditations-Folder

CHAPTER TWELVE

Journey to the West

Gaining Heart Certainty is your journey to the West. The modality for this journey is unconditional love and compassion for all beings, and it will strengthen your authority while you help others serve the highest good for all. Simply listening, loving, caring, and nurturing the connection to the Infinity-Fire is the embodiment of a journeyman traveling West. This journey starts with leading yourself and ridding your being of baggage so that you can help others. Sometimes our mission of helping others is so simple, small, or obvious, but that doesn't matter! Even one random act of kindness can change the world! Traveling into the metaphorical West is the journey of a leader and leadership takes self-reflection, courage, and ownership of everything that happens inside your space. At its core, leadership is about seeing obstacles and struggles as opportunities and then taking advantage of those opportunities to create solutions for yourself and others that embody the highest good for all. Only a select few journey to the West, and that is okay. Just remember that being a leader is about leading yourself before you lead others.

This journey goes beyond the Heart-Fire and leads you to your River of Life. To truly give unconditional love and compassion to the world, a Chātra needs to access their own River of Life. Your River of Life can recharge you if you've given too much and are feeling drained, or even if you need some peace and quiet in your sacred space.

So, what exactly is a River of Life? Imagine the most special and personal place in the universe and go beyond it. Your river of life is where you bathe in sacred healing water and let go of all lower vibrations; it is heaven in your mind and a place where you can take refuge whenever you want. (It can be a place from your past or future, or somewhere you completely make up!) The most important quality of your River of Life is that it is a place of healing and perfection; it needs to be somewhere to which you can travel when you feel "off" so that you can have all of your original instructions instantly restored. (Think of computer coding as your original instructions: when the code becomes broken and corrupted, the system will malfunction. This exact process occurs when your human systems start to become corrupted from negative emotions!) You can travel to your River of Life for healing of the mind, body, and spirit whenever you need to restore your system to the perfection it was meant to be. You may find there is a time when you need to reset your original instructions to what you and the Infinity-Fire originally agreed upon, and traveling to your River of Life for a lengthy visit will recalibrate your entire system.

CONCLUSION

Combining all your Heart-Fire skills will integrate your entire nervous system into a single sense organ. The end-state of this approach is to stop seeing only with your eyes and instead to pay attention to the invisible forces with which you interact. Your mind naturally tries to condense twenty million bits of data that streams into your nervous system into forty bits of information. When this occurs, there is a massive amount of distortion, deletions, and generalizations, and your sense of reality becomes skewed from true reality. To truly see is to see with your heart and feel the universe in which you live as a vibrational field. When you arrive at a place on this journey that you couldn't have possibly imagined, keep going! Whatever you think you are, you are so much more than that.

After my healing crisis and personal transformation, I started on a journey to become a life coach. I didn't have a plan—all I knew is that I untied the boat during my visionary state, and I was going to sail in a direction. I knew the seas would get rough, and the winds would change, but if I followed the stars and the light of the moon during the darkest nights, I would find my way. During an acupuncture session with my doctor, he mentioned that I should go to NLP training with the

Empowerment Partnership. As soon as he told me about it, my heart sang with excitement. I knew I had to do this training and it became a heart calling. I immediately scheduled the training for six months from that day and I could not wait!

About three months before the NLP training, I was lying in bed extremely sick with the flu. It was beating me down with a high fever, so I decided to move to the couch and listen to some music to try to meditate the fever away. Thankfully, I fell asleep during my meditation, but I woke up in the middle of the night with a voice inside my being intensely saying, "You will write a book!" This thought was accompanied by an image, so I grabbed my journal and started drawing and writing in the dark. I fell asleep again, and when I woke up in the morning, I saw my writings and drawings. The picture I had drawn looked like a crystal with energy waves flowing through it. I started writing my book that very morning and the flu was gone by that evening. I became very focused on writing for the next few months, so I didn't think much of my drawing until I was sitting in the NLP conference. We were watching a presentation and one of the slides that appeared on the screen was almost *exactly* the same image that I had drawn months before. My jaw dropped and I started laughing right there in the middle of the session. That moment solidified to me that I needed to follow my heart, and that's when I knew that NLP and breakthrough sessions were my soul's purpose.

Here I am, right now in this very moment, sensing direction with my heart.

In the end, reforming an alliance with the Infinity-Fire and allowing a union to form between yourself and the divine will bring you the spiritual power of unconditional love and compassionate action. Unconditional love is the fabric of the universe and compassion is love plus understanding driving kindness. The vibrations of unconditional love and compassion are the force that manifests your soul's contract. Finding your soul's purpose and following a path of fulfillment is accomplished by consulting your Heart-Fire every day.

Your Heart-Fire method is simple: connect, remember, surrender, receive, and ask a question. While in deep meditation, this process of connecting, remembering, surrendering, receiving, and asking a question is ancient wisdom. No matter the way you view the higher power, this is a method to connect with a higher consciousness that will show you unconditional love and compassion. If you constantly tap into the Infinity-Fire, detoxify your heart, and follow your Heart-Fire, you will experience miracles in your life.

You will undergo positive changes in terms of improved moods, better health, increased happiness, unconditional love for others, compassionate actions, and most of all, an influx of spiritual power that will manifest your highest potential. Manifesting your soul's purpose and experiencing true fulfillment is the end-state of the

Heart-Fire method. So, go out there and remember your Sacred Ancestry, and always come back to the realization that you are a being of light channeled into the actions of a beautiful human.

Where am I on my Heart-Fire path? I am currently in the youth stages of my journey South toward my ultimate Western trajectory of becoming a spiritual elder. I have learned so much from studying wildland fire on the physical landscape and I now understand myself in a deeper way as a result. Even still, I still have so much more to learn!

There are also a million words in my future because I cannot stop writing and helping others with spoken and written word. Keep an eye out for my other titles, *Why Science Likes Me, Overcome Anxiety Like a Hero*, and *Internal Leadership. Why Science Likes Me* was originally part of this book, but it is more powerful when separately read. I am humbled by my Heart-Fire every day because I have to practice Heart-Fire Embrace to lead myself into the deepest unconditional love and compassionate action. I ask myself three questions every day: *Am I writing? Am I helping people? Am I experiencing joy?* If I answer, "Yes" to these questions, I am fulfilling my soul's purpose. I feel so blessed to have a fulfilling soul's purpose through my writing, so thank you for reading!

As you move forward, remember your spiritual nature is pure consciousness experiencing a human body. This will dissolve negative vibrations and low, dense emotions into the highest possible vibrations. Detoxifying your heart and filling it up with divine vibrations will manifest miracles in your life! You will be able to manifest your soul's contract through a Heart-Fire awakening by following the steps I have outlined in this book. With the Heart-Fire method, you will be able to sense danger, find nourishment, illuminate your soul's purpose, and walk in the direction of fulfillment, one step at a time.

Practicing the Heart-Fire method will allow you to learn from the divine and tap into the ancient wisdom of your higher-self. A Heart-Fire path is individual and specific, so follow your gut! You have all the wisdom inside of you that you will ever need if you just listen. Go forth and vibrate unconditional love and compassion into the world and see what happens! In doing this, I challenge you to carry out at least one act of kindness every day.

Many Blessings!

[1] "Forced Vibration - The Physics Classroom." https://www.physicsclassroom.com/class/sound/Lesson-4/Forced-Vibration. Accessed 16 Jun. 2019.

[2] "New Scientific Breakthrough Proves Why Acupuncture Works ..." https://www.actcm.edu/blog/acupuncture/new-scientific-breakthrough-proves-why-acupuncture-works/. Accessed 12 Jun. 2019.

[3] "Understanding Emotions in Traditional Chinese Medicine." 20 Mar. 2019, https://www.verywellmind.com/emotions-in-traditional-chinese-medicine-88196. Accessed 12 Jul. 2019.

[4] "Pattern of disharmony between the heart and ... - ScienceDirect.com." https://www.sciencedirect.com/science/article/pii/S2095754817302193. Accessed 5 Jun. 2019.

[5] "The Seven Emotions | HowStuffWorks - Health | HowStuffWorks." https://health.howstuffworks.com/wellness/natural-

medicine/chinese/traditional-chinese-medicine-causes-of-illness6.htm

6 "What is Life Between Lives Hypnotherapy?." https://www.newtoninstitute.org/about-tni/what-is-life-between-lives/. Accessed 21 Sep. 2019.

7 "Common Denominators Of Fire Behavior On Tragedy Fires ..." https://www.nwcg.gov/committee/6mfs/common-denominators-of-fire-behavior-on-tragedy-fires. Accessed 4 Jan. 2020.

8 "Gut Feelings–the "Second Brain" in Our ... - Scientific American." 1 May. 2015, https://www.scientificamerican.com/article/gut-feelings-the-second-brain-in-our-gastrointestinal-systems-excerpt/?fbclid=IwAR2wHm9aZuWjQ0hbPGaQtS9biw38xpbEmBl4etZvdowQ8VE4kzNCOIEErKk. Accessed 12 Jun. 2019.

9 "The Art Of War (9781599869773): Sun Tzu: Books - Amazon.com." https://www.amazon.com/Art-War-Sun-Tzu/dp/1599869772. Accessed 17 Jun. 2019.

10 "The effects of grounding (earthing) on ..." 24 Mar. 2015,

https://www.ncbi.nlm.nih.gov/pmc/articles/PMC43782
97/. Accessed 24 Jan. 2020.

[11] "Your gut is directly connected to your brain, by a
newly discovered ..." 20 Sep. 2018,
https://www.sciencemag.org/news/2018/09/your-gut-
directly-connected-your-brain-newly-discovered-neuron-
circuit. Accessed 5 Jun. 2019.

[12] "(PDF) Neurocardiology Anatomical and Functional
Principles | Jaime ..."
https://www.academia.edu/37169649/Neurocardiology
_Anatomical_and_Functional_Principles.   Accessed   5
Jun. 2019.

[13] "Our Thoughts Don't Create Reality: The Law of
Attraction Clarified ..." 7 Nov. 2015,
http://www.elephantjournal.com/2015/11/our-
thoughts-dont-create-reality-the-law-of-attraction-
clarified/. Accessed 13 Jun. 2019.

[14] "Quick   Coherence®   Technique - HeartMath."
https://www.heartmath.com/quick-coherence-
technique/. Accessed 13 Jun. 2019.

[15] "Take a Deep Breath: The Physiology of Slow Deep
Breathing."
https://www.grc.com/health/research/Breathing/The%

20Physiology%20of%20Slow%20Deep%20Breathing.pd
f. Accessed 10 Jun. 2019.

[16] "The experiments of Masaru Emoto with emotional imprinting of water." 13 May. 2018,
https://www.researchgate.net/profile/M_Pitkanen/proj
ect/Topological-Geometrodynamics-
TGD/attachment/5b0b8a16b53d2f63c3ce72b0/AS:631
123189186560@1527482902589/download/Emoto.pdf?
context=ProjectUpdatesLog. Accessed 10 Jun. 2019.

[17] "Tap Water Quality | US drinking water quality data by zip code." https://mytapwater.org/. Accessed 10 Jun. 2019.

[18] "SuperWellness: Become Your Own Best Healer; The Revolutionary ..."
https://www.amazon.com/SuperWellness-
Revolutionary-Formula-Creating-
Vibrant/dp/0999436015. Accessed 10 Jun. 2019.

[19] "A Pisgah Sight of Palestine and the Confines Thereof: With the History ..." https://www.amazon.com/Pisgah-
Sight-Palestine-Confines-Thereof/dp/1149132078.
Accessed 14 Jun. 2019.

CPSIA information can be obtained
at www.ICGtesting.com
Printed in the USA
LVHW101031061222
734675LV00005B/293